30 Day Whole Food Slow Cooker Challenge

Whole Food Recipes for your Slow Cooker – Quick and Easy Chef Approved Whole Food Recipes for Weight Loss

Table of Contents

Introduction

I want to thank you for choosing this book, '30 Day Whole Food Slow Cooker Challenge - Whole Food Recipes for Your Slow Cooker – Quick and Easy Chef Approved Whole Food Recipes for Weight Loss'

Losing weight is not an easy task and understandably so. It requires dedication and the maintenance of a rigorous exercise routine. But considering the time crunch faced by people these days, it is next to impossible to follow an effective diet or an exercise routine.

One good way of dealing with this is by turning to a source of inspiration that can help you kick-start your weight loss journey. This book promises to do just that and will guide you through an effective meal plan triggered to generate weight loss which is sure to get you results.

The book focuses on the consumption of whole foods, which provide the body with a plethora of health benefits. You will feel great about yourself and notice a big change in your overall wellbeing.

To make your journey easy, we have collated many recipes for you that are made using whole food ingredients. The recipes will be prepared using a slow cooker - an appliance that helps in the retention of nutrients and also makes meals tastier as well as helping you to cook without having to slog in front of a hot stove for hours.

The ingredients used in these recipes are easily available and can be sourced from your local farmers' market. I have tried to use budget friendly ingredients that are not just easy on the pocket but extremely healthy and that will help you stay healthy and lose weight at the same time.

I thank you once again for choosing this book and hope you attain the body of your dreams.

Good luck!

Chapter 1: What is the Whole Foods 30 Day Challenge?

To begin with, we will try to explain the 30-day challenge, and answer a few basic questions.

What are whole foods?

Whole foods refer to foods that are unrefined and unprocessed. These foods are plant-based ingredients that have not undergone any form of chemical processing.

Whole foods are considered to be extremely healthy, as they are not treated with chemicals and preservatives. They are free from processing, which can affect their structure and make them less nutritious. Although whole foods now tend to incorporate animal derivatives, the term is mostly used to refer to plant-based foods such as leaves, fruits, vegetables, grains, seeds etc.

Basically, anything that is unrefined, unprocessed and free from chemicals will count as whole foods.

What is the whole foods 30-day challenge?

The whole foods 30-day challenge is one where you are required to consume whole foods for 30 days at a stretch, and all other types of food will be kicked out of your diet.

The aim of the diet is to help you lose weight and develop a lean body. However, that does not form the main goal of the diet, as it focuses on other aspects of wellbeing such as sleep enhancement, glowing skin, shinier nails, stronger bones etc.

Once the 30 days have passed, you will be allowed to reintroduce all those foods that were eliminated from your diet. This will also give you an opportunity to find those foods that you are allergic to, and remove them from your diet on a permanent basis.

What is processing and refining?

Most factory-based foods undergo processing and refining in order to extend their shelf life. These include the likes of canned foods, packaged foods etc. Companies tend to add chemicals in order to preserve the foods and enhance their flavor. In doing so, they end up adding ingredients that can prove to be health hazards. Sugars, fats, sodium and preservatives remain some of the most dreaded ingredients that go into these processed foods. Not only will they have an ill effect on the body but also on the mind, and therefore, are best avoided.

What processed foods should be avoided?

According to the Whole food diet, you are required to cut out all processed and junk foods from your diet. This includes the likes of instant noodles, flavored nuts, frozen meals, sauces and condiments, popcorn, chocolates, processed dry fruits and granola bars to name just a few. You must develop the habit of reading food labels. There will be some that will claim to use whole foods but who lie about it. If you spot sugars, saturated fat or any other such ingredient then it is best to drop it.

How effective is the diet?

The diet can be extremely effective if you manage to follow it diligently. It is not a fad diet that you take up and leave half way through just because you think it is not working. You are required to stick with it for at least 30 days and then slowly return to trying to incorporate these changes in your regular diet. If you are in a hurry to see results, then you will end up disliking the diet. You have to remain patient and carry on with it for 30 days or more.

Are you allowed to consume cheat meals?

No. You are not allowed to consume any cheat meals including healthier versions of your favorite junk foods, prepared using healthier ingredients. Therefore, homemade, healthy pancakes, pizzas or burgers are off limits.

Can I continue with the diet after 30 days?

Yes. If you wish to continue with the diet after the 30 days are over, then you can do so. You do not have to discontinue it and can carry on until you are satisfied with the results. If you like, you can reintroduce a few animal derivatives such as lean meats and dairy products. You will have the choice to turn the whole foods diet into a lifestyle choice.

Will I require supplements?

Yes, you might require a few supplements if you plan on continuing with the diet for long. Since it eliminates dairy products, you might have to consume calcium supplements to make up for it. Similarly, you might require other supplements depending on whatever is lacking in your body. Your doctor will be able to suggest the best supplements for you.

Are there any age restrictions?

No. There are no age restrictions and the diet is safe to be adopted by people of all ages. Right from youngsters to elders, anybody interested in enhancing their overall health can take up the whole foods 30-day challenge.

These form a few of the basic questions asked on the topic and hope you found your answers.

Chapter 2: Foods to Eat and Foods to Avoid

In the previous chapter, we looked at the basics of the whole foods 30 days challenge and in this chapter, we will look at the foods that can and cannot be consumed on the diet.

Foods to eat

As per the whole foods diet, you are allowed to consume only plant-based foods that are free from processing. They are as follows.

Vegetables

Root vegetables

You are allowed to consume all types of root vegetables including carrots, potatoes, beetroots, parsnips, celery, asparagus, radish, Kohlrabi, daikon, turnip etc.

Bulbs

All bulb vegetables such as onions, garlic, chives, leeks, scallions etc

Stems

All stem vegetables such as leeks, broccoli, water spinach, Malabar spinach etc.

Leaves

All leafy vegetables such as spinach, kale, arugula, mustard greens and collard greens, Swiss chard, Romaine lettuce etc

Flowers

Flowers such as cauliflower, broccoli, artichokes, cauliflower etc

Try not to overcook the vegetables and cook them using the slow cooker as much as possible.

Fruits

You can consume all types of fruits including watermelon, cantaloupe, tomatoes, grapes, apples, strawberries, pears, peach, banana, cherry, pineapple, mangoes, grapefruit, avocado, papaya, apricot, cranberry, pomegranate, passion fruit, pomelo etc.

It would be best to buy your vegetables from organic markets as they have produce free of chemicals and additives. If there is no such market in your area then consider looking online.

Grains

You are allowed to consume all types of whole grains including rye, barley, brown rice etc. Make sure they are free from processing. Avoid buying products that mention "refined" on the label.

Nuts

Nuts including pecans, walnuts, almonds, cashews etc. can be consumed on the diet. Refrain from consuming processed nuts as they can contain preservatives.

Mushrooms

All types of mushrooms including Portobello mushrooms, white buttons, shiitake etc. can be consumed. Make sure you buy fresh mushrooms and avoid frozen ones.

Legumes

You can consume the likes of beans, peas, lentils such as yellow lentils, green lentils etc. You must avoid buying canned beans as they can contain preservatives. Buy whole beans and soak them overnight to help them cook better.

Foods to avoid

Here is a list of foods to avoid on the diet.

Animal based foods

Diets rich in animal-based proteins are considered to be unhealthy. People fail to associate a protein rich diet with health risks such as coronary heart disease and cancer. There is also the risk of developing Type 2 diabetes and, therefore, it is advisable to stop, or control intake of animal-based foods. The recommended dose of protein is 10% but people end up consuming almost twice that amount. It, therefore, becomes essential to control the intake of animal products. They will also contain less fiber as compared to whole foods thereby making it all the more important to avoid consumption. You must also avoid derivatives such as eggs and dairy.

Junk food

You must completely eliminate junk foods from your diet. Remember that these foods can negatively impact your body and offset various illnesses. Junk foods will not contain essential fiber that is required to maintain a healthy digestive tract. They will also not contain any of the vital nutrients that are required to develop a healthy body. Instead, they will contain chemicals and preservatives that can lead to cell damage and mental illnesses. Therefore, all types of junk foods including pizzas, burgers, fries etc. should be eliminated from the diet.

Processed foods

Most people do not realize that processed foods are just as dangerous as junk foods. These foods are those that come out of a packet and contain lots of chemicals and preservatives. You must avoid consuming them at all costs as they can lead to health complications. Do not buy chips, biscuits, cakes and other packaged foods from supermarkets. Avoid eating baked goods as they can contain a lot of refined sugar. If you already have these lying in your pantry then clear them out before getting started on the diet as that way you can avoid the temptation of consuming them. You must also avoid aerated and caffeinated drinks, as they can be full of sugar.

Dairy

It is advisable to avoid consuming dairy products. Many people believe that dairy products are important to maintain bone health but this is not true. You do not need dairy products such as milk, cheese and yogurt to enhance good health. In fact, they can cause hormonal issues that can affect breast and prostate health. It is, therefore, best to avoid consuming dairy products as much as possible and instead settle for alternatives like nut milk and cheese.

Fats/oils

Fats and oils should be avoided as much as possible. Although there are claims that olive oil is the safest oil to consume, it is still full of calories and poor in nutrition. So you do not have the liberty to fry foods in olive oil just because you think it is healthier. You can use it to drizzle over salads or shallow fry foods. Avoid fats such as butter, cheese, clarified butter etc.

Alcohol

You have to avoid consuming alcohol as much as possible. Alcohol can cause your body more damage than processed and junk foods combined. Not only will it affect your liver but also digestive tract and heart. If you have a drinking problem then consider visiting a therapist. Inform your friends and family about your diet so that they do not force you to drink. Carry a bottle of juice with you so that you can drink from it and not feel awkward at parties and dinners.

Smoking/drugs

You must avoid smoking and drugs, as smoking can negatively impact your body. Kick the habit as soon as you can and avoid doing drugs. It is best to eliminate those friends from your group who smoke or do drugs as they can encourage you to join them. Cut back on it slowly as stopping once and for all can confuse your body and kick start a craving.

These form the different foods that you have to avoid while on the whole foods 30 days diet.

Chapter 3: Benefits of the Whole Foods 30 Days Challenge

Here are some of the health benefits provided by the whole foods 30 days challenge.

Energy levels

The whole foods 30-day challenge is sure to leave you feeling extremely energetic. You will not feel tired at the end of day's work and have enough energy to perform routine tasks. It will not be like your regular surge and drop in energy that is commonly seen with other diets, and you will have the chance to maintain consistent energy throughout the course of the day. The vegetables and fruits will fill you up with ample energy that is enough to help you power through your day.

Sleep

Sleep is a very important aspect of life but often neglected. Most people end up compromising on their sleep and indulge in activities such as watching television or using their cell phones. However, the whole foods diet will ensure that sleep is automatically induced and will help you to sleep better, and for longer hours. You will also not get up during the night and have the chance to clock 8 to 10 hours of continuous sleep, thereby increasing your body's healing capacity.

Digestion

It is important to improve your digestive capacity and, in turn, your metabolism. The whole foods 30 days challenge is one such diet that helps in increasing your digestive power. It includes foods that are rich in fiber, which help in digestion and elimination. You will not feel bloated or heavy or complain about flatulence. The food you eat will easily digest and pass through without getting stuck in your digestive system. Your liver and gut will also have it easy thereby enhancing your overall wellbeing.

Immunity

By cutting out junk and processed foods, you have the chance to enhance immunity. The liver is where your first line of defense against germs and so strengthening it will work towards helping you enhance your immunity. With Whole food diet, your liver will not feel burdened and function smoothly.

Thinking

With the help of the diet, you will find it easier to think clearly. You do not have to worry about brain fogging and have the chance to remain alert and awake. This will increase your productivity and enhance your overall level of confidence. You will not feel confused and be in a position to take firm decisions.

Mood

Your mood will greatly improve through the consumption of whole foods. You will feel amazing at yourself and avoid getting angry or worked up. Good mood will ensure that you develop a better bond with friends and family members, thereby enhancing your mental wellbeing.

Stress

With the Whole food diet, you will experience less episodes of stress and anxiety. You will not feel anxious, and will be in a position to avoid getting into stressful situations. The diet is full of brain-healthy ingredients such as omega 3 fatty acids that will cut down on the level of cortisol in your brain and increase serotonin. You will feel happier and healthier within a week of switching over to the diet.

Heart health

The elimination of animal-based ingredients will help towards increasing heart health. Omega 3 fatty acids will also help towards enhancing heart health. Your bad cholesterol will reduce while good cholesterol will increase. Exercising on a regular basis will further improve the state of your heart.

Hydration

It is important to remain as hydrated as possible in order to maintain cell health. The diet will make sure that you drink 8 to 10 glasses of water a day and remain well hydrated. You need not consume just water and can switch it up with fruit juices, fruit infused water etc. Make sure you do not add any sugar, honey or artificial sweetener to the drinks and keep it natural.

Taste

One of the biggest disadvantages of consuming a diet rich in junk and processed foods is that it tends to alter people's taste. This can be solved by cutting out such foods and consuming foods that are whole and free from processing. You will begin to enjoy your meals and be in a position to appreciate its positive effects on your body. You will also have the chance to avoid adding any sauces and condiments, as the meals themselves will be extremely tasty.

Eat less

It is important to eat within your limit and not overeat. Many people tend to get carried away and end up eating more than their capacity. But with the Whole food diet, it will be easier for you to control your hunger and ensure that you eat within your limit. You will feel full and content after your meals and not feel the need to settle for a snack in between.

Skin

With the Whole food diet, your skin will start to glow and you will experience less breakouts. You will find it easier to control oily skin and maintain a consistent glow. It is also a good way to avoid the appearance of fine lines and wrinkles and reverse some of the damage caused by the sun.

Hair

The Whole food diet incorporates foods that are rich in vitamin E, thereby enhancing hair health. You will see that your hair is shinier and stronger and experience lesser issues such as hair fall and split ends. You will also find it easier to manage frizz and maintain healthy, shiny hair.

Nails and teeth

The Whole food diet will ensure better nail and teeth health. Your nails will not chip as easily and your teeth will remain strong. You will have lesser dental complaints and be able to grow your nails long.

Lean muscles

The Whole food diet will help you develop lean muscles. Lean muscles are those that are not burned away easily. These muscles can only be developed through the consumption of foods rich in proteins such as chickpeas, mushrooms etc. If you plan on getting started with a muscular body then the Whole food diet is sure to push you in the right direction.

Confidence

Since your overall health will improve, you will feel more confident about yourself.

These form just a few of the many health benefits that the Whole food diet provides.

Chapter 4: Why Use A Slow Cooker With This?

The health benefits provided by the Whole food diet can be further enhanced through the use of a slow cooker. In this chapter, we will look at a slow cooker in detail.

What is a slow cooker?

A slow cooker is a device that cooks food at a slower pace, so the nutrition in the food remains intact. A slow cooker can be used to cook a variety of meals including meats, vegetables, grains, legumes etc. It looks like a rice cooker, all you have to do is add all the ingredients into the cooker and set it to cook over a desired period of time. This ensures that the nutritional value of the food remains intact.

A slow cooker will make your life easier as you do not have to slog in the kitchen to prepare healthy meals. All you have to do is add the ingredients into the cooker and it will take care of the rest.

Why use a slow cooker?

Here is why you should be using a slow cooker.

Simple to use

The slow cooker is easy to use and can be used by just about anyone. You can go through the instructional manual provided by the company to understand how the cooker works. Once you start using it, it will get easier for you to cook your everyday meals. You can choose between automatic and manual models, however, most cookers these days come with both options. You can also use your cooker as a regular pressure cooker thereby making it a versatile appliance to have in your kitchen. You will find it easier to cook your meals without having to slog through it.

Time saving

You can save a lot of time by making use of the slow cooker. You do not have to worry about sautéing, braising, etc. You can simply toss all the ingredients into the cooker and wait for them to cook out. You can add the ingredients at night and have your meals ready by morning.

Cost effective

One of the advantages of using a slow cooker is that you can prepare heartier meals with lesser ingredients. The cooker tends to hold on to the water content in the vegetables thereby making them more filling. You can easily cut down on the amount of vegetables that you cook with and ensure you make the most of them.

Safe to use

The slow cooker is extremely safe to use and can be operated by just about anyone. Right from women to men to even children, the slow cooker makes for an ideal appliance to cook with. You don't have to worry about the cooker heating up too much and burning your fingers. It comes with insulation so that the outsides do not get too hot.

Easy to maintain

With the slow cooker, you do not have to worry about having to work with too many utensils. You just need the cooker and a spatula and you are good to go. All you have to do is add the ingredients, sauté if you like, add liquid and cover the cooker. Once done, you can empty the cooker and wash the inner vessel. You can save on cooking as well as cleaning time just by making use of a slow cooker.

Yogurt making

You can easily make yogurt using a slow cooker. All you have to do is add soymilk or any other nut-based milk to the cooker and bring to a boil. Once done, let is sit for 2 hours. Take a little milk into a bowl and add some yogurt. Whisk it well and add it back to the cooker. Place it in a dark place for 8 to 9 hours and your yogurt should be ready.

Benefits of using a slow cooker

Here are some of the benefits of cooking in a slow cooker.

Nutrients

The slow cooker works in such a way that it maintains the nutritional content of food. The cooker cooks food at a slower pace and ensures that the heat does not burn away nutrition. You can choose an 8 or 12-hour setting to cook food in order to ensure that the nutrition remains intact.

Moisture content

The moisture content of the vegetables remains intact. This means that your body gets more water and your cells feel replenished. Your skin will feel moisturized and begin to glow. You will see a big difference in your overall appearance.

Taste

Your food will taste better when cooked in a slow cooker. The cooker ensures the slow release of juices from the vegetables thereby making it tastier. Your children will enjoy the meals as well and not complain about having cut out junk and processed foods from the diet.

Slow cooker cooking tips

- The Slow Cooker will retain the moisture present in vegetables and therefore, it is best to add just a little water while cooking. If you end up adding too much then it will overcook the veggies making them soggy. However, you will need to add at least some water as otherwise; the cooker will not produce steam. Add about half a cup of water so that the vegetables have a chance to sweat it out. If you do end up with too much water then set the slow cooker on high let the water get absorbed with the heat.

- It is best to sauté vegetables and herbs before cooking in a slow cooker. This will enhance their flavor and taste.

- Cut all your vegetables to the same size. Having uniform sizes will ensure that they cook consistently and you have a tasty meal. You can arrange the cut vegetables at the bottom of the cooker and cook it to your liking.

- Layer delicate vegetables such as tomatoes, spinach on top of other vegetables. This will ensure that they do not wilt. They can also be added about 30 minutes before switching off the cooker in order to preserve their flavor.

- It is best to precook pasta and rice and then add to the slow cooker as cooking them in the crockpot can make them sticky.

- You can use your slow cooker to keep the dish warm. It can also be used to heat up a meal.

- In case you feel like something is burning, immediately switch off the slow cooker and open it.

- Keep your slow cooker pushed away from edges as tumbling over can damage it.

Chapter 5- Enhancing The Diet's Output

Here are a few things that you can do to enhance the output of the whole food diet plan.

Stop counting

It will be best to stop counting your calorie intake and checking your weight loss. The Whole food diet is not like your regular diet where you will notice a difference in your weight within a month or so. The change will be gradual but lasting. Once you start losing weight, it will continue until you reach the desired goal. Check your weight before starting out with the diet and check again once the 30 days are up. You will notice a slight difference, which will be an indication of the weight loss that is to come.

Calculate proteins/fat

It will be a good idea to calculate your protein and fat intake per meal. Many people make the mistake of calculating just the carbohydrate intake and forgo calculating other nutrients. You will have to check from time to time, whether you are consuming the recommended amount or going overboard. Consider consulting a dietician, who will tell you exactly how much proteins and fat you have to consume in a day. Ask him to help you come up with meal plans that will provide you the recommended doses of vital nutrients.

Drink fluids

It is important to increase your fluid intake. Liquids, especially water, have the capacity of melting down fat and eliminating from the body. It also keeps your body hydrated and energetic. If you work out, then it will be important to increase the water intake by 40%. Carry a bottle of water with you and drink every half an hour or so. If it gets monotonous then switch to fruit infused water. Cut up a few lemons and mint leaves and add to your regular bottle of water. Shake it vigorously and consume every few hours. You can also switch to fruit juices but ensure that no extra sugar or honey is added in.

Carbs before workout

One golden rule to follow while on the diet is to consume carbs just before working out. Doing so will help you lose weight at a faster pace and also ensure that any extra carbs consumed during the meal is burned away. It will be a good idea to eat a carb rich meal in the afternoon and avoid having one at night. You can hit the gym in the evening or late afternoon. You can have a light, protein-rich snack post workout so that your muscles feel nourished.

Smaller meals

It will be a good idea to split your regular meals into 5 or 6 smaller meals. By doing so, you will give your body the chance to break down the food in a better manner. The nutrients will have more time to reach the desired organs thereby enhancing your overall health. But remember that your regular 3 meals will have to be cut down into 6 meals and not 6 regular meals. Following this routine will also ensure that you avoid the temptation of consuming snacks in between your meals.

Increase fiber

It is vital to increase the fiber content in your meals. Fiber is an important nutrient required by the body to remain healthy. It helps in loosening fat and eliminating it from the body. The digestive tract puts in a lot more effort to digest fiber thereby burning away calories. Try to consume at least 35 grams of fiber (men) and 25 grams (women) per day, so that your body is able to digest food in a better manner.

Natural supplements

You can turn to natural supplements to help you enhance your overall health. Natural supplements contain vital nutrients that are essential for the body and add back whatever your diet is unable to provide. There are many types of supplements to choose from such as ginseng, ashwagandha etc. You can do a little research on what supplements are good for you, and consume them to supplement the diet.

Superfoods

There are several whole foods that are super foods, capable of enhancing good health. These foods can increase your overall well being and add to the diet's effects on your body. Some of them include the likes of garlic, turmeric, wheat, berries, avocados, tomatoes etc. Consuming these on a daily basis can turn your health around and put you on the right track to sustained weight loss.

Carrying out these simple steps can enhance your diet's output. But do not limit yourself to just these and do whatever you think will add to your gains.

Daily schedule to follow

Here is a daily schedule that you can follow.

Healthy breakfast

Start your day off with a healthy breakfast. Include lots of fruits and vegetables and also fibrous foods. Prepare a fresh breakfast every day and avoid eating yesterday's leftovers. A bowl of oatmeal with some fresh fruits will make for a great breakfast option. Follow it up with a tall glass of juice. Take your daily supplements and consume a tall glass of water.

Meditate

Spend some time in the morning meditating so that you can control stress. Find a quiet corner and start meditating. Meditate for at least 15 minutes every day.

Carb-rich lunch

Consume a carbohydrate-rich meal in the afternoon. Prepare a carb-rich lunch and take it to the office. Remember that this meal should have slightly more carbs than the other meals and not too much.

Workout

Work out early in the evening so that your body has the chance to burn the carbs away. Try to exercise for at least 30 minutes a day, 5 days a week. Try to mix it up so that it does not get monotonous.

Light dinner

Finish the day by having a light dinner. It should not be heavy as that can interfere with your sleep. Do not drink too much water before bedtime. You can consume a glass of warm soymilk before sleeping to sleep well.

Sleep early

Try to sleep earlier than usual, so you can get ample sleep and also wake up early, with enough time for other activities like workout, meditation and a breakfast.

Chapter 6: Slow Cooker Breakfast Recipes

Honey Vanilla Multigrain Hot Cereal

Serves: 6

Ingredients:

- 3 cups plain almond milk, unsweetened
- 2 tablespoons honey
- ¼ teaspoon fine sea salt
- 6 tablespoons pearl barley, rinsed
- 6 tablespoons steel-cut oats
- ¼ cup quinoa, rinsed
- 1 cup coconut water
- ¾ teaspoon vanilla extract

Method:

1. Add almond milk, coconut water, vanilla and honey into the slow cooker. Whisk well.
2. Add rest of the ingredients and stir.
3. Close the lid. Select 'Low' option and set the timer for 5-7 hours.
4. Serve hot.
5. Unused cereal can be stored in an airtight container in the refrigerator for 5 days.

Coconut Cranberry Quinoa

Serves: 8

Ingredients:

- 6 cups coconut water
- 2 tablespoons honey
- 2 cups quinoa, rinsed
- ¼ cup coconut flakes
- ½ cup cranberries, dried
- ¼ cup almonds, sliced
- 2 teaspoons vanilla extract

Method:

1. Add coconut water, vanilla and honey into the slow cooker. Whisk well.
2. Add rest of the ingredients and stir.
3. Close the lid. Select 'Low' option and set the timer for 4 hours. Or select 'High' for 2 hours.
4. Serve hot.
5. Unused cereal can be stored in an airtight container in the refrigerator for 4- 5 days.

Pumpkin Pie Oatmeal

Serves: 12

Ingredients:

- 2 cups steel cut oats
- 4 cups low fat milk
- 4 cups water
- 2 cups canned pumpkin puree
- 2 teaspoons vanilla extract
- ½ teaspoon salt
- 2 teaspoons pumpkin pie spice
- A few drops of liquid Stevia or ½ cup agave nectar

Method:

1. Add all the ingredients except Stevia into the slow cooker. Add agave nectar if using. Mix well.
2. Close the lid. Select 'Low' option and set the timer for 6-7 hours. Add Stevia if using at this stage.
3. Serve hot.
4. Unused cereal can be stored in an airtight container in the refrigerator for 2-3 days.

Caramelized Apple-Oatmeal

Serves: 3

Ingredients:

- 3-4 apples, cored, peeled, diced
- 1 cup whole milk
- 1 cup water
- 1 cup rolled oats
- 6 tablespoons brown sugar
- ¼ teaspoon freshly ground nutmeg
- 2 teaspoons ground cinnamon
- 1 tablespoon lemon juice
- 1 egg (optional)
- A pinch sea salt
- Cooking spray

Method:

1. Spray some cooking spray the inside of the slow cooker.
2. Place a layer of apples at the bottom of the slow cooker, followed by brown sugar, cinnamon, nutmeg, salt, lemon juice and oats. Do not stir.
3. Whisk together egg and milk and pour over the layers. Do not stir. Pour only milk if not using egg.
4. Close the lid. Select 'Low' option and set the timer for 6-9 hours depending on how you like the apples to be browned.
5. Serve hot.
6. Unused cereal can be stored in an airtight container in the refrigerator for 2-3 days.

Oatmeal with Vegetables

Serves: 4-6

Ingredients:

- 1 small zucchini, peeled, grated
- 1 large carrot, peeled, grated
- 1 cup steel cut oats
- ½ cup pecans, chopped
- 1/8 teaspoon ground cloves
- 1/8 teaspoon ground nutmeg
- 1 teaspoon ground cinnamon
- 2 teaspoons vanilla extract
- 3 cups vanilla flavored milk of your choice (dairy or non-dairy)
- 4 tablespoons agave nectar or maple syrup

Method:

1. Add all the ingredients except pecans to the slow cooker and stir.
2. Close the lid. Select 'Low' option and set the timer for 7-8 hours.
3. Add pecans before serving. You can add more milk if you desire.
4. Serve hot.
5. Unused cereal can be stored in an airtight container in the refrigerator for 2-3 days.

Apple Granola Crumble

Serves: 6

Ingredients:

- 4 Granny Smith apples, peeled, cored, chopped into chunks
- ¼ cup maple syrup
- 2 cups granola cereal of your choice
- 4 tablespoons butter
- ½ cup apple juice
- 1 teaspoon ground nutmeg
- 2 teaspoons ground cinnamon

Method:

1. Add all the ingredients except Stevia into the slow cooker. Add agave nectar if using. Mix well.
2. Close the lid. Select 'Low' option and set the timer for 4 hours.
3. Serve hot.
4. Unused cereal can be stored in an airtight container in the refrigerator for 2-3 days.

Fruited Irish Oatmeal

Serves: 4-5

- 1 cup Irish steel cut oats
- 2 tablespoons dried cranberries
- 2 tablespoons dried apricots, chopped
- 2 tablespoons golden raisins
- 1 teaspoon ground cinnamon
- A pinch salt
- 2 tablespoons maple syrup + extra to serve
- ½ cup apple juice
- 2 ½ cups water
- Milk to serve
- Chopped almonds or pecans, toasted to serve

Method:

1. Add all the ingredients except pecans and milk into the slow cooker and stir.
2. Close the lid. Select 'Low' option and set the timer for 6-7 hours.
3. Add pecans or almonds and milk before serving.
4. Serve hot.
5. Unused cereal can be stored in an airtight container in the refrigerator for 2-3 days.

Creamy Homemade Yogurt

Ingredients:

- 1 gallon milk
- 12 ounces plain yogurt with live cultures
- 3 teaspoons vanilla extract (optional)
- 1 cup maple syrup or honey (optional)

Method:

1. Pour milk into the slow cooker
2. Close the lid. Select 'Low' option and set the timer for 2-3 hours or until it reaches a temperature between 150 to 175 degree F. Switch off the cooker.
3. Cover and set aside until the milk cools down to 110 degree F.
4. Take out about a cup of milk from the cooker and pour into a bowl. Add the live culture. Whisk well and add it to the pot. Stir well.
5. For flavored yogurt, add vanilla and honey if using at this stage. You can use any other flavoring of your choice.
6. Cover the slow cooker with a large blanket and set aside for 8 - 12 hours or until set. This step is important or else the yogurt will not set.
7. When set, set aside some of the yogurt as the live culture for your next batch of yogurt.
8. Chill for at least a couple of hours and serve.

Huevos Rancheros

Serves: 4-5

Ingredients:

- 5 eggs
- 6 ounces cheddar cheese, shredded
- 1 clove garlic, minced
- ½ cup half and half
- 2 ounces canned chopped green chilies, drained
- 5 ounces taco sauce
- ¼ teaspoon ancho chili powder
- ¼ teaspoon black pepper powder
- Salt to taste
- 1 avocado, peeled, pitted, sliced
- 2 scallions, sliced
- 2 tablespoons fresh cilantro, chopped
- Juice of a lime
- Cooking spray

Method:

1. Spray the inside of the slow cooker with cooking spray.
2. Add eggs and half and half into a bowl and whisk well. Add 4 ounces of cheese, pepper powder, salt, and chili powder. Add garlic and green chilies. Fold gently and transfer into the slow cooker.
3. Close the lid. Select 'Low' option and set the timer for 2 hours.
4. Uncover and check after around 1-½ hours of cooking. If it is not set, then cook for another 30 minutes or until the eggs are set.
5. Pour taco sauce on top of the set eggs and spread evenly all over. Sprinkle the remaining cheese all over the sauce.
6. Close the lid. Select 'Low' option and set the timer for 15 minutes.
7. Slice into 4-5 wedges.
8. Warm tortillas as per the instructions on the package. Place a wedge on each of the tortillas. Sprinkle scallions and cilantro. Place avocado slices and finally sprinkle lemon juice and serve.

Spinach and Mushroom Casserole

Serves: 4

Ingredients:

- 8 eggs, whisked
- ¼ teaspoon salt or to taste
- 1 tablespoon red onion, minced
- 1/3 cup milk
- 1/3 cup sundried tomatoes
- 1 ½ cups spinach
- ¾ cup portabella mushrooms, sliced
- 1 teaspoon garlic, minced
- ½ teaspoon black pepper powder or to taste
- 1/3 cup feta cheese, crumbled

Method:

1. Add eggs, milk, salt and pepper to a large bowl. Whisk until well combined. Add sun-dried tomatoes, mushrooms, garlic, onion and spinach. Mix lightly and pour into the slow cooker.
2. Sprinkle cheese over it.
3. Close the lid. Select 'Low' option and set the timer for 4-6 hours.
4. Serve hot.

Broccoli, Bacon and Bell Pepper Casserole

Serves: 4

Ingredients:

- 15 ounces frozen hash brown potatoes
- 2 strips turkey bacon, cut into small pieces, cooked, drained (optional)
- 1 small onion, diced
- 4 ounces cheddar cheese
- 1 small green bell pepper, diced
- 1 small red bell pepper, diced
- A large pinch salt
- Pepper powder to taste
- 2 egg whites
- 6 tablespoons milk
- 2 cloves garlic, minced or garlic salt to taste
- ½ small head broccoli, chopped into small pieces
- 1 teaspoon ground mustard
- 4 eggs
- Salt to taste
- Pepper powder to taste
- Cooking spray

Method:

1. Whisk together in a bowl, whites, garlic salt, salt, mustard and pepper in a bowl.
2. Grease the bottom of the slow cooker with cooking spray.
3. Place half of the hash brown potatoes at the bottom of the slow cooker. Sprinkle half of each, onions, bell peppers, broccoli and cheese.
4. Repeat the above step with the remaining half.
5. Pour beaten egg mixture over it.
6. Close the lid. Select 'Low' option and set the timer for 4-6 hours.
7. Serve hot.

3 Cheese Shrimp and Grits

Serves: 3

Ingredients:

- ¾ cup quick cooking grits
- 3 cups chicken stock or broth
- ½ tablespoon onion powder
- ½ tablespoon garlic powder
- ½ teaspoon dried thyme or 1 teaspoon fresh thyme, minced
- 1 pound raw shrimp
- ½ cup cheddar cheese
- ¼ cup cream cheese
- 1 cup parmesan + extra for garnishing
- 1 teaspoon hot sauce (optional)
- 2 teaspoons fresh chives
- 1 scallions, chopped for garnishing
- ¼ cup cream or half and half

Method:

1. Add all the ingredients except cream, shrimp and scallions into the slow cooker and stir.
2. Close the lid. Select 'Low' option and set the timer for 3 hours.
3. Add shrimp and half and half. Cook on 'Low' option for 30 minutes.
4. Garnish with cheese and serve hot.

Mexican Fiesta Breakfast Frittata

Servings: 9-10

Ingredients:

- 12 large eggs
- 1/3 cup sun dried tomatoes (not oil packed)
- 2 ounces canned fire roasted green chilies or 2 jalapeños, deseeded, finely chopped
- 3 teaspoons skim milk
- 1 medium red bell pepper, chopped
- 1 cup green onions, chopped
- 1 ½ cups chunky salsa
- 1 ½ teaspoons Mexican oregano
- 12 ounces low fat cheddar cheese, shredded
- Salt to taste
- Pepper to taste
- ¼ cup fresh cilantro
- Avocado, peeled, pitted, sliced
- 1 scallions, sliced
- Cooking spray

Method:

1. Spray the inside of the slow cooker with cooking spray.
2. Whisk together in a bowl, eggs, salt, pepper, and milk. Add cheese and stir.
3. Select 'Low' option and allow the cooker to heat.
4. Add onions, red bell pepper, sun dried tomatoes, oregano and chilies and stir. Let it heat.
5. Pour the egg mixture over the vegetables in the cooker.
6. Close the lid. Select 'Low' option and set the timer for 3 hours or until a toothpick when inserted in the center comes out clean.
7. Garnish with cilantro, scallion, and avocado.
8. Slice and serve with salsa.

Crust less Spinach and Feta Quiche

Serves: 4

Ingredients:

- 8 eggs
- 20 ounces frozen chopped spinach, thawed
- 4 cups milk
- 4 cloves garlic, minced
- 8 ounces feta cheese, crumbled
- Salt to taste
- Pepper to taste

Method:

1. Whisk together eggs and milk in a bowl. Add rest of the ingredients and stir.
2. Spray inside of the slow cooker with cooking spray. Pour the mixture into it.
3. Close the lid. Select 'Low' option and set the timer for 3 hours or until a toothpick when inserted in the center comes out clean.

Sausage and Apple Bread Pudding

Serves: 2

Ingredients:

- 2 ¼ cups whole wheat bread (French or Italian bread), cubed
- ¼ teaspoon ground allspice
- ½ teaspoon ground cinnamon
- 6 ounces sausages, cooked, crumbled
- 2 medium apples, peeled, cored, chopped
- 1/8 teaspoon salt
- 2 tablespoons firmly packed light brown sugar
- 2 tablespoons maple syrup
- 1 cup milk or soy milk
- Cooking spray

Method:

1. Grease inside of the slow cooker with a little cooking spray. Place half the bread cubes at the bottom and press.
2. Mix together rest of the ingredients except sausages in a bowl. Pour half this mixture over the bread in the cooker. Press lightly.
3. Place half the sausages over it. Next place the remaining bread. Pour the remaining apple mixture over it. Press again lightly.
4. Close the lid. Select 'Low' option and set the timer for 6 hours.
5. Serve hot.

Quinoa Breakfast Casserole

Serves: 2-3

Ingredients:

- ¼ cup quinoa, rinsed
- 3 large eggs
- ¼ cup frozen chopped spinach
- ¾ cup milk
- 4-5 grape tomatoes, halved
- Salt to taste
- Pepper powder to taste
- 2 tablespoons parmesan cheese, shredded
- 2 tablespoons cheddar cheese
- Cooking spray

Method:

1. Spray the inside of the slow cooker with cooking spray.
2. Whisk together eggs, milk, salt and pepper. Add quinoa and whisk well.
3. Add spinach, tomatoes, and half the cheese. Transfer into cooker. Sprinkle remaining cheese on top.
4. Close the lid. Select 'High' option and set the timer for 2 hours or until set.
5. Serve hot.

Chili Verde Breakfast Lasagna

Serves: 6

Ingredients:

- 1 ½ pounds bulk breakfast sausage
- 2 fresh jalapeño peppers, finely chopped
- 8 eggs, lightly beaten
- 1 large green bell pepper, finely chopped
- 1 tablespoon vegetable oil
- 3 green onions, sliced
- 1 teaspoon salt
- 1 teaspoon ground cumin
- 3 cups cheddar cheese
- Sour cream to serve (optional)
- 1 ½ jars (16 ounces each) salsa Verde
- 1/3 cup fresh cilantro or parsley, chopped + extra to garnish
- 12 corn tortillas
- Cooking spray

Method:

1. Spray the inside of the slow cooker with cooking spray. Place a disposable liner at the bottom of the cooker.
2. Place a skillet over medium heat. Add sausages and cook until brown, breaking it simultaneously as it cooks. Drain the excess fat.
3. Add bell pepper and jalapeños and sauté for a minute. Transfer into a bowl and set aside.
4. Place the skillet back over medium heat. Add oil. When the oil is heated, eggs and scramble it. Transfer it into the bowl of sausages.
5. Add green onions, cilantro, salt, and cumin powder. Stir well.
6. Place 3 tortillas at the bottom of the pot. Overlap the tortillas if necessary. Spread 1/3 of the sausage mixture over it. Spread ½ jar salsa Verde followed by 1-cup cheese.
7. Repeat the above layer twice.
8. Close the lid. Select 'Low' option and set the timer for 3-4 hours.
   Switch off the cooker when the timer goes off. Let the lasagna remain in the pot for 15 minutes. If possible, slowly remove the disposable liner.
9. Sprinkle cilantro over it. Slice and serve with a dollop of sour cream.

Pumpkin Bread

Serves:

Ingredients:

- 4 cups + 2 tablespoons whole wheat flour
- 1 ½ teaspoons ground cinnamon
- 2 teaspoons baking soda
- 1 cup olive oil or canola oil
- 4 eggs
- 2 teaspoons vanilla extract
- 1 cup walnuts, chopped
- 1 teaspoon salt
- 1 1/3 cups maple syrup
- 2 tablespoons milk
- 2 cups pumpkin puree
- 1 cup dark chocolate chips
- Cooking spray

Method:

1. Select 'High' and close the lid. Let the cooker heat.
2. Grease a loaf pan that fits into your slow cooker with cooking spray. If you have a small cooker, then grease 2 loaf pans. Sprinkle 1-2 tablespoons flour on the bottom as well as the sides. Drop off the excess flour.
3. Add all the dry ingredients into a large mixing bowl. Mix well. Add oil, eggs, maple syrup, milk and vanilla and whisk until well combined and free from lumps.
4. Add pumpkin puree, walnuts and chocolate chips and mix until well combined.
5. Pour the batter into the prepared loaf pan.
6. Close the lid. Select 'High' option and set the timer for 2 hours or until a toothpick when inserted in the center comes out clean.
7. Cool on a wire rack.
8. Slice and serve.

Apple Honey Tea

Serves: 12 cups

Ingredients:

- 24 ounces canned frozen apple juice or cider concentrate, thawed
- 2 tablespoons honey
- 4 tablespoons instant tea powder
- 1 teaspoon ground cinnamon

Method:

1. Add all the ingredients into the slow cooker and stir.
2. Close the lid. Select 'Low' option and set the timer for 1-2 hours.
3. Whisk well, pour into mugs and serve hot.

Pumpkin Spice White Hot Chocolate

Serves: 6

Ingredients:

- 6 cups whole milk
- 1/3 cup pumpkin puree
- 3 teaspoons vanilla extract
- 1 ½ teaspoons freshly grated nutmeg + extra to garnish
- Whipped cream topping (optional)
- 1 ½ cups white chocolate chips
- 6 sticks cinnamon (3 inches each)+ extra to garnish
- ¼ teaspoon ground ginger

Method:

1. Add all the ingredients except whipped cream topping into the slow cooker and stir.
2. Close the lid. Select 'Low' option and set the timer for 2-3 hours. Stir every 10 minutes for the first hour of cooking. Stir every half hour during the remaining time.
3. Whisk well and pour into mugs.
4. Top with whipped cream. Sprinkle nutmeg. Insert a cinnamon stick in each mug.
5. Serve.

Chai Tea

Serves: 8

Ingredients:

- 8 cups milk
- ½ cup canned pumpkin
- 2 teaspoons pumpkin spice
- 3 cups brewed black tea
- 8 tablespoons coconut sugar or raw sugar
- 4 teaspoons vanilla extract
- Ground cinnamon to serve
- Whipped cream to serve

Method:

1. Add all the ingredients except cinnamon and whipped cream into the slow cooker and whisk well.
2. Close the lid. Select 'Low' option and set the timer for 2 hours.
3. Whisk well and pour into mugs.
4. Add a dollop of whipped cream. Sprinkle cinnamon and serve.

Maple Pumpkin Spice Latte

Serves: 7

Ingredients:

- 2 cups espresso coffee
- 6 tablespoons canned, plain pumpkin
- 1 tablespoon vanilla extract
- 4 cups milk of your choice (dairy or non dairy)
- 6 tablespoons maple syrup or to taste
- 1 tablespoon pumpkin pie spice or to taste

Method:

1. Add all the ingredients into the slow cooker and stir.
2. Close the lid. Select 'Low' option and set the timer for 2-3 hours.
3. Whisk well and pour into mugs.
4. Pour into mugs and serve hot.

Veggie Juice

Ingredients:

- 23 ounces vegetable juice
- 1 tablespoon lemon juice
- 1 small stalk celery, halved crosswise
- 1 teaspoon Worcestershire sauce
- 1 tablespoon packed brown sugar

Method:

1. Add all the ingredients into the slow cooker and whisk well.
2. Close the lid. Select 'Low' option and set the timer for 4-5 hours or on 'High' for 2 – 2 ½ hours.
3. Discard celery, pour into mugs and serve hot garnished with fresh celery sticks.

Chapter 7: Slow Cooker Appetizer Recipes

French Dip

Serves: 4

Ingredients:

- 2 pounds pot roast
- 4 cloves garlic, peeled
- 16 ounces beef broth
- 1 small onion, quartered
- 2 teaspoons ground mustard
- 2 teaspoons Italian seasoning
- Salt to taste
- Pepper to taste

Method:

1. Add all the ingredients into the slow cooker.
2. Close the lid. Select 'Low' option and set the timer for 7-8 hours or on 'High' for 2 ½ - 3 hours.
3. Remove the cooked pot roast and place on your cutting board.
4. When cool enough to handle, shred with a pair of forks. Add it back to the pot, reheat and serve with mini bread rolls.

Corn and Jalapeno Dip

Serves: 4

Ingredients:

- 1 ½ cans (15.25 ounce each) whole corn kernels, drained
- ¼ cup sour cream
- 2 slices bacon, chopped
- ½ cup pepper Jack cheese, shredded
- 4 ounce cream cheese, chopped into cubes
- 2 tablespoons parmesan cheese, grated
- 1 jalapeno, deseeded and sliced
- 1 tablespoon fresh chives, chopped
- Kosher salt to taste
- Freshly ground black pepper to taste

Method:

1. Place a skillet over medium heat. Add bacon and cook until crisp. Remove and set aside on a plate lined with paper towels. Drain the fat that is remaining in the skillet.
2. Add all the ingredients except cream cheese and chives to the slow cooker. Stir. Place the cream cheese cubes over it.
3. Close the lid. Select 'Low' option and set the timer for 2 hours.
4. Uncover, stir and select 'High' and cook for 15 minutes.
5. Garnish with chives and bacon and serve.

Buffalo Chicken Dip

Serves: 5

Ingredients:

- 1 package (8 ounce) cream cheese, softened
- ½ cup hot sauce
- ½ cup mozzarella cheese, shredded
- ½ cup deli rotisserie chicken, shredded
- ½ cup blue cheese dressing or ranch dressing
- ¼ cup blue cheese, crumbled

For serving: (Use any)

- Celery sticks
- Toasted bread stick
- Crackers

Method:

1. Place all the ingredients in the slow cooker in layers with mozzarella and blue cheese right on top.
2. Close the lid. Select 'Low' option and set the timer for 2 hours.
3. Serve warm with toasted bread sticks or celery sticks or crackers.

Pepperoni Dip

Serves: 5-6

Ingredients:

- 16 ounces cream cheese
- 14 ounces sliced pepperoni
- 21 ounces cream of celery soup

For serving: (Use any)

- Celery sticks
- Toasted bread stick
- Crackers

Method:

1. Add all the ingredients into the slow cooker.
2. Close the lid. Select 'Low' option and set the timer for 4 hours or on 'High' for 2 hours.
3. Stir and serve with celery sticks or toasted bread sticks or crackers.

Reuben Dip

Serves: 4-6

Ingredients:

- 2 cups sour cream
- 2 cups Swiss cheese, shredded
- 2 cups sauerkraut, drained, chopped
- 8 ounces corned beef, shredded
- 16 ounces cream cheese
- 4 tablespoons thousand island dressing

Method:

1. Add all the ingredients into the slow cooker.
2. Close the lid. Select 'Low' option and set the timer for 1-1 ½ hours.
3. Serve warm with rye bread slices.

Chicken Nachos

Serves: 6-8

Ingredients:

- 3 chicken breasts, boneless, skinless
- 2 teaspoons taco seasoning or to taste
- ½ bag tortilla chips or as required
- 8 ounces salsa
- 1 cup cheddar cheese, shredded

For topping (optional):

- ¼ cup black olives, sliced
- 2 green onions, thinly sliced
- Guacamole as required
- 1/4 cup sour cream
- Salsa as required
- 1 jalapeño pepper, thinly sliced
- Cooking spray

Method:

1. Spray the inside of the slow cooker with cooking spray.
2. Lay the chicken in the pot and pour salsa over it. Sprinkle seasoning.
3. Close the lid. Select 'Low' option and set the timer for 8 hours or on 'High' for 4 hours.
4. When done, remove the chicken with a slotted spoon. When cool enough to handle, shred the chicken with a pair of forks.
5. Place the chips on a large serving platter. Place a bit of the chicken over each of the chips. Place the toppings over it and serve.

Mushroom Garlic Crostini

Serves: 6

Ingredients:

- ½ pound small white mushroom, cleaned, trimmed
- 1 tablespoon extra virgin olive oil
- 1 tablespoon fresh parsley
- 1 teaspoon balsamic vinegar
- 12 crostini
- 4 cloves garlic, roasted
- 1 large shallot, finely chopped
- 2 tablespoons white wine
- 1 tablespoon heavy cream
- Salt to taste
- Freshly ground pepper to taste
- Soft goat's cheese, crumbled, as required

Method:

1. Add garlic, shallots, mushroom and oil into the slow cooker.
2. Close the lid. Select 'Low' option and set the timer for 8 hours or on 'High' for 4 hours or until the mushrooms are tender.
3. Strain by passing through a strainer. The cooked liquid can be used in some other dish.
4. Transfer the strained mushroom and garlic into a food processor. Add parsley and pulse until the mushrooms are finely chopped. It should not be made into a puree.
5. Add cream, salt, pepper and vinegar and pulse for 2-3 seconds until the mixture is well combined.
6. Place the crostini on a baking sheet. Spread the mixture on each of the crostini. Top with goat's cheese.
7. Bake in a preheated oven at 375 F for a few minutes until the cheese melts and is brown as per your desire.
8. Serve hot.

BBQ Chicken Drummies

Serves: 4

Ingredients:

- 1 ½ pounds frozen chicken drummies, thawed, pat dried
- 2 tablespoons honey
- ¾ cup barbecue sauce
- 1 tablespoon chili sauce
- 2 cloves garlic, minced
- Pepper to taste

Method:

1. Place the drummies in a baking dish.
2. Broil for 8-10 minutes. Transfer into the slow cooker.
3. Add rest of the ingredients and stir.
4. Close the lid. Select 'Low' and set the timer for 4-5 hours or on 'High' for 2 -2 ½ hours or until the chicken is tender.

Party Potatoes with Creamy Aioli

Serves: 4

Ingredients:

- 1 pound tiny new potatoes, halve them if they are slightly bigger
- ¼ cup low sodium chicken or vegetable broth
- 1 medium red onion, cut into thin wedges
- 2 cloves garlic, minced
- 1 green onion, thinly sliced
- Pepper to taste
- Salt to taste
- 2 teaspoons prepared horseradish
- 2 teaspoons fresh dill, chopped or ½ teaspoon dried dill
- ¼ teaspoon salt or to taste
- ¼ teaspoon smoked or regular paprika
- 4 ounces light sour cream
- 2 teaspoons onions, finely chopped
- Cooking spray

Method:

1. Spray the inside of the slow cooker with cooking spray.
2. Add onions and potatoes into the slow cooker.
3. Add broth, half the garlic and paprika into a bowl and mix well.
4. Close the lid. Select 'Low' and set the timer for 6-7 hours or on 'High' for 3 -3 ½ hours or until the potatoes are tender.
5. Meanwhile make the aioli as follows: Add rest of the ingredients into a bowl and stir.
6. Cover the bowl with cling wrap and chill until use.
7. When the potatoes are cooked, transfer into a serving bowl. Add salt, pepper and green onions and toss well.
8. Serve potatoes with aioli. It can also be served at room temperature.

Barbecue Chickpeas

Serves: 5-6

Ingredients:

- 1 ½ cans (15 ounces each) chickpeas, rinsed, drained
- ½ teaspoon onion powder
- ½ teaspoon salt
- ½ teaspoon garlic powder
- ½ teaspoon smoked paprika
- 3 ounces tomato paste
- 1 tablespoon blackstrap molasses
- ¼ cup water or as required
- 1 tablespoon maple syrup or honey
- 2 tablespoons apple cider vinegar

Method:

1. Add all the ingredients into the slow cooker. Add water as required. Less for dry chickpeas and more for a little gravy.
2. Close the lid. Select 'High' option and set the timer for 2 ½ -3 hours.

Crab Spread

Serves: 4

Ingredients:

- ½ pound lump crab meat, discard shell bits and cartilage
- 6 tablespoons mayonnaise
- 1 small onion, minced
- 4 ounces cream cheese, softened
- 4 teaspoons apple juice
- Salt to taste
- Pepper powder to taste

Method:

1. Add all the ingredients into the slow cooker and stir.
2. Close the lid. Select 'Low' option and set the timer for 4 hours.
3. Serve within 2 hours of cooking.

Chapter 8: Slow Cooker Soup, Stew and Chili Recipes

Wonder Soup

Serves: 8

Ingredients:

- 1 head cabbage, chopped
- 2 cups onions, chopped
- 2 green bell peppers, chopped
- 2 cups celery, chopped
- 2 cups carrots, chopped
- 6 cloves garlic, minced
- 2 cans basil, oregano, garlic diced tomatoes
- 2 teaspoons basil
- Pepper to taste
- Salt to taste
- 8 cups chicken broth
- 2 teaspoons dried oregano
- 1 teaspoon red pepper flakes
- 1 tablespoon olive oil

Method:

1. Place a skillet over medium heat. Add oil. When the oil is heated, add onions and sauté until translucent.
2. Transfer into the slow cooker.
3. Add rest of the ingredients and stir.
4. Close the lid. Select 'Low' and set the timer for 1 ½ - 2 hours.
5. Taste and adjust the seasonings if necessary.
6. Ladle into soup bowls and serve.

Pureed Broccoli Soup

Serves: 3

Ingredients:

- 4 cups fresh broccoli, cut into florets
- 1 small stalk celery, chopped
- 1 small onion, chopped
- 1 clove garlic, chopped
- 1 cup water
- ¼ cup half and half or sour cream or low fat yogurt to serve
- 1 teaspoon fresh thyme or parsley, chopped
- 2 cups vegetable or chicken broth
- Salt to taste
- Freshly ground pepper to taste
- 2 teaspoons extra virgin olive oil
- 2 teaspoons butter

Method:

1. Place a skillet over medium heat. Add oil and butter. When butter melts, add onions and celery and sauté for a couple of minutes.
2. Add garlic and thyme and sauté for a few seconds until fragrant. Transfer into the slow cooker.
3. Add all the ingredients except half and half or sour cream or yogurt to the cooker and stir.
4. Close the lid. Select 'Low' and set the timer for 1 ½ - 2 hours or until the broccoli is tender.
5. Taste and adjust the seasonings if necessary.
6. Ladle into soup bowls and serve.
7. Blend the contents with an immersion blender or in a blender until smooth.
8. Simmer for a while.
9. Ladle into soup bowls.
10. Serve garnished with half and half or sour cream or yogurt.

Lentil and Ham Soup

Serves: 2

Ingredients:

- ½ cup dried lentils, rinsed, soaked in water for a couple of hours
- ½ cup carrots, chopped
- 2 cloves garlic, minced
- ½ cup celery, chopped
- ½ cup onions, chopped
- ¾ cup cooked ham
- 3 cups chicken broth or any other broth
- 3 tablespoons tomato sauce
- 1 bay leaf
- ¼ teaspoon dried oregano
- ¼ teaspoon dried thyme
- ¼ teaspoon dried basil
- Salt to taste
- Pepper to taste
- 1 cup water

Method:

1. Add all the ingredients to the slow cooker and mix well.
2. Close the lid. Select 'Low' and set the timer for 6-7 hours or on 'High' for 3 -3 ½ hours.
3. If you find your soup too thick, add more broth or water and heat thoroughly.
4. Taste and adjust the seasonings if necessary. Discard the bay leaf.
5. Ladle into soup bowls and serve.

Sweet Potato, Apple and Turmeric Soup

Serves: 3-4

Ingredients:

- 1 large onion, cut into 2 inch pieces
- ¾ pound potato, cut into 2 inch pieces
- 3 pounds sweet potatoes, cut into 2 inch pieces
- 1 ½ pounds apple, cored, cut into 2 inches
- 1 ½ teaspoons turmeric
- 1 ½ tablespoons apple cider vinegar
- Freshly ground pepper to taste
- 6 cloves garlic, peeled, smashed
- 3 cups vegetable stock or chicken stock
- 1 ½ cups coconut milk
- Kosher salt to taste

Method:

1. Add onion, garlic, potatoes, sweet potatoes, apples, turmeric salt and stock into the slow cooker and stir.
2. Close the lid. Select 'Low' and set the timer for 5-6 hours or on 'High' for 3 -3 ½ hours or until tender.
3. Add apple cider vinegar and coconut milk and stir. Blend with an immersion blender until smooth and creamy. You can also blend in a blender.
4. Ladle into soup bowls and serve.

Spicy Black Bean Soup

Serves: 3

Ingredients:

- ½ pound dry black beans, rinsed soaked in water overnight
- 3 cups broth
- 1 jalapeño peppers, chopped
- ¼ tablespoon chili powder
- ¼ teaspoon garlic powder
- ½ teaspoon cumin powder
- ½ teaspoon cayenne pepper
- ¼ teaspoon hot sauce
- Salt to taste
- Pepper powder to taste

Method:

1. Add all the ingredients to the slow cooker.
2. Close the lid. Select 'High' option and set the timer for 4 hours.
3. Next select 'Low' option and set the timer for 2 hours.
4. If you find the soup too thick, add some more water and cook for 15 minutes.
5. Taste and adjust the seasonings if necessary.
6. Ladle into soup bowls and serve.

Creamy Potato and Corn Chowder

Serves: 3-4

Ingredients:

- 1 medium russet potatoes, diced
- 1 ½ cups frozen corn, thawed, divided
- 1 medium sweet potato, cubed
- 1 cup chicken stock or vegetable
- 1 onion, chopped
- ¼ teaspoon garlic powder or 2 cloves, minced
- ½ teaspoon dried basil or 1 tablespoon fresh basil, chopped
- ½ tablespoon white wine vinegar
- Salt to taste
- Pepper powder to taste
- ½ cup coconut milk
- 1 tablespoon unsalted butter
- 1 scallion, thinly sliced

Method:

1. Add potato, sweet potato, half the corn, stock, onion, garlic and salt into the slow cooker. Mix well.
2. Close the lid. Select 'Low' option and set the timer for 5-6 hours or on 'High' for 2-3 hours or until tender.
3. Add remaining corn, vinegar and coconut milk and stir.
4. Ladle into soup bowls and serve garnished with basil and scallions and serve.

Farmer's Mexican Chicken Soup

Serves: 2-3

Ingredients:

- 1 pound chicken, skinless, chopped into pieces
- 1 cup chicken stock or broth
- 1 cup water
- 1 carrots peeled, sliced
- 1 small yellow onion, chopped
- 1 poblano pepper, chopped
- 2 cloves garlic, thinly sliced
- 3 small zucchinis, chopped
- 10-12 cherry tomatoes, halved
- 2 cups kale or Swiss chard, discard hard stems and ribs, torn
- ½ cup tomato juice or tomato sauce
- ½ teaspoon cumin
- ½ teaspoon ground coriander
- ¼ teaspoon garlic powder
- ¼ teaspoon chili powder
- 1 tablespoon sea salt
- Juice of a lemon
- ¼ cup cilantro, chopped
- 2 cups water

To serve (optional): Use any of them

- Cheddar cheese chips
- Scallion, thinly sliced
- Cilantro, chopped
- Avocado slices
- Hot sauce

Method:

1. Add chicken, onion, carrots, tomato sauce, spices, salt, water and stock into the slow cooker.
2. Close the lid. Select 'Low' option and set the timer for 5-6 hours or on 'High' for 3 -3 ½ hours or until tender.
3. Remove the chicken pieces from the pot, remove the bone and shred the chicken with a fork.
4. Add the shredded chicken back to the pot. Add rest of the ingredients and stir.
5. Cook on 'Low' for 40-60 minutes or until the vegetables are tender.
6. Meanwhile make the cheddar cheese chips as follows: Shred some cheddar cheese and place on a lined baking sheet. Bake at 400 F for 6-7 minutes. Remove from the oven and let it cool completely.
7. Ladle into individual soup bowls and serve garnished with any toppings mentioned above and serve.

Tomato Beef and Macaroni Soup

Serves: 4

Ingredients:

- ½ pound extra lean ground beef
- ½ cup frozen spinach
- ½ cup red bell pepper, chopped
- ¾ cup whole grain elbow macaroni, uncooked
- 1 clove garlic, minced
- 1 medium onion, chopped
- 1 cup low sodium beef broth
- 13 ounces canned tomato pasta sauce
- Salt to taste
- Pepper to taste
- ½ teaspoon dried oregano
- ½ tablespoon dried basil
- ¼ teaspoon crushed red pepper flakes
- 14 ounces canned diced tomatoes

Method:

1. Place a skillet over medium heat. Add beef and sauté until brown. Add garlic and sauté for a couple of minutes. Transfer into the slow cooker.
2. Add rest of the ingredients except macaroni and spinach into the cooker and stir.
3. Close the lid. Select 'Low' option and set the timer for 5-6 hours or on 'High' for 3 -3 ½ hours or until tender.
4. Add macaroni and spinach. Cover and cook on 'High' for 15 minutes or until macaroni is al dente.
5. Ladle into soup bowls and serve.

Chicken, Black Bean and Quinoa Stew

Serves: 4

Ingredients:

- 1 can (15 ounces) black beans, drained, rinsed (you can use cooked black beans)
- 2 ounces canned, fire roasted diced green chilies
- 1 can (14.5 ounces) fire roasted diced tomatoes, divided
- 1 small yellow onion, chopped
- 2 large carrots, chopped
- 2 cups low sodium chicken stock
- 1 teaspoon kosher salt or to taste
- ½ teaspoon garlic powder
- ½ teaspoon ground cumin
- 1 pound chicken breasts or thighs, skinless, boneless
- Juice of ½ lime
- Hot sauce to taste
- 6 tablespoons quinoa, rinsed
- 1 avocado, peeled, pitted, sliced
- 2 tablespoons fresh cilantro, chopped

Method:

1. Add black beans, ½ the tomatoes, garlic, powder, onion, carrot, salt, cumin, stock and green chilies into the slow cooker. Stir well.
2. Add chicken and stir again.
3. Close the lid. Select 'Low' option and set the timer for 6 hours or on 'High' for 3-4 hours or until tender.
4. Remove chicken with a slotted spoon. Place on your cutting board. When cool enough to handle, shred with a pair of forks.
5. Add it back to the slow cooker. Add quinoa and stir.
6. Close the lid. Select 'Low' and set the timer for 45- 60 minutes or until tender.
7. Add remaining tomatoes and lime juice and stir.
8. Taste and adjust the seasoning if necessary.
9. Ladle into soup bowls. Garnish with cilantro. Top with avocado slices and serve.

Irish Lamb Stew

Serves: 4

Ingredients:

- 1 pound leg of lamb, boneless, trimmed of fat, cut into 1 inch pieces
- 2 large leeks, white parts only, thinly sliced
- ¾ pound white potatoes, peeled, cut into 1 inch pieces
- 2 large carrots, peeled, cut into 1 inch pieces
- 1 stalk celery, thinly sliced
- 1 cup chicken broth
- 3 teaspoons fresh thyme, chopped
- 2 tablespoons fresh parsley, chopped
- Salt to taste
- Pepper powder to taste

Method:

1. Add all the ingredients except parsley to the slow cooker.
2. Close the lid. Select 'Low' option and set the timer for 7-8 hours or on 'High' for 3 ½ -4 hours or until tender.
3. When done add parsley, mix well
4. Ladle into soup bowls and serve.

Autumn Vegetable Beef Stew

Serves: 8-12

Ingredients:

- 2 -3 pounds lean stew beef meat, cubed
- 4 cups beef broth
- 4 strips bacon, chopped
- 10 medium potatoes, diced
- 4 ribs celery, thinly sliced
- 4 medium carrots, thinly sliced
- 3 cups rutabaga, chopped
- 2 large onions, chopped
- 2 bay leaves
- Freshly ground pepper to taste
- Salt to taste
- 1 teaspoon dried rosemary, crushed
- 4 tablespoons flour mixed with ½ cup water
- A handful parsley, chopped to garnish

Method:

1. Place a skillet over medium heat. Add onions, bacon and beef and sauté for a few minutes until the beef is not pink any more.
2. Transfer into the slow cooker.
3. Add rest of the ingredients except the flour mixture. Mix well.
4. Close the lid. Select 'Low' option and set the timer for 7-8 hours or on 'High' for 3 ½ -4 hours or until tender.
5. Add flour mixture stir well.
6. Select 'High' and set the timer for 15-20 minutes. Stir when done.
7. Taste and adjust the seasonings if necessary.
8. Ladle into soup bowls. Garnish with parsley and serve.

Simple Hamburger Stew

Serves: 8-12

Ingredients:

- 2 pounds 90% lean ground beef
- 4 stalks celery, sliced
- 2 large onions, chopped
- 4 large potatoes, sliced
- 4 medium carrots, sliced
- 3 cups frozen peas, thawed
- 2 cans (8 ounces each) tomato sauce
- 2 cans (14.5 ounces each) diced tomatoes with juice
- 4 teaspoons Italian seasoning
- Salt to taste
- Pepper powder to taste

Method:

1. Place a skillet over medium heat. Add ground beef and cook until brown. Transfer into the slow cooker.
2. Add rest of the ingredients except peas to the cooker and stir.
3. Close the lid. Select 'Low' option and set the timer for 6-8 hours or on 'High' for 3 - 4 hours or until potatoes and meat are tender.
4. Add the peas during the last hour of cooking and stir.
5. Stir in between a couple of times while it is cooking.
6. Taste and adjust the seasonings if necessary.
7. Ladle into soup bowls. Serve warm with toasted bread.

Butternut Squash, Kale and Quinoa Stew

Serves: 8

Ingredients:

- 2 large yellow onions, finely chopped
- 6 cloves garlic, minced, finely grated
- 1 teaspoon smoked paprika
- 2 cans (14.5 ounces each) diced tomatoes
- ¼ cup dry quinoa, rinsed
- 2 teaspoons white wine vinegar
- 6 cups butternut squash, cubed
- 2 teaspoons ground cumin
- 2 teaspoons salt or to taste
- 8 cups vegetable broth
- 6 cups kale, discard hard stems and ribs, torn
- Extra virgin olive oil to drizzle
- Freshly ground pepper to taste

Method:

1. Add onion, garlic, paprika, butternut squash, tomatoes, salt, broth and quinoa into the slow cooker. Mix well.
2. Close the lid. Select 'Low' option and set the timer for 6-8 hours or on 'High' for 4 hours.
3. Add kale and cook for 30 minutes or until kale wilts.
4. Add vinegar and stir.
5. Taste and adjust the seasonings and vinegar if necessary.
6. Ladle into soup bowls. Sprinkle pepper. Drizzle oil and serve.

Vegetarian Chili

Serves: 4-6

Ingredients:

- ½ cup quinoa or farro, uncooked
- 2 cloves garlic, minced
- 7.5 ounces light red kidney beans, rinsed, drained
- 1 can (15 ounce) dark red kidney beans, rinsed, drained
- 2 ounces canned chopped green chilies
- 1 can (14 ounce) diced tomatoes
- 1 chipotle chili in adobo sauce, chopped
- 1 small onion, chopped
- 2 ½ cups vegetable stock
- 1 tablespoon chili powder
- ½ tablespoon ground cumin
- ½ teaspoon sugar
- ½ teaspoon black pepper powder
- ½ teaspoon salt or to taste
- Cheddar cheese, shredded to serve
- 2 green onions, sliced to serve

Method:

1. Add all the ingredients except cheese and green onions to the slow cooker.
2. Close the lid. Select 'Low' option and set the timer for 6-8 hours or on 'High' for 3 ½ hours.
3. Taste and adjust the seasonings if necessary.
4. Ladle into bowls. Garnish with cheese and green onions and serve.

The Ultimate Chili

Serves: 4

Ingredients:

- ¾ pound lean ground beef
- 2 cans (14.5 ounces each) Mexican style stewed tomatoes
- 2 cans (15 ounces each) dark red kidney beans
- 2 tablespoons red wine vinegar
- 1/4 cup red wine
- 1 small red bell pepper, chopped
- 1 stalk celery, chopped
- 1 tablespoon chili powder or to taste
- 1/2 teaspoon dried basil
- 1/2 teaspoon dried parsley
- 1/2 teaspoon ground cumin
- 1/2 teaspoon Worcestershire sauce
- Salt and pepper to taste
- Cooking spray

Method:

1. Place a skillet over medium heat. Add ground beef and cook until brown.
2. Add all the ingredients except red wine to the slow cooker and stir.
3. Close the lid. Select 'Low' option and set the timer for 6-8 hours or on 'High' for 3-4 hours.
4. Add wine after 4 hours of cooking. Stir and continue cooking until the timer goes off.

Easy Chili

Serves: 3

Ingredients:

- ¾ pound turkey
- 1 can (15 ounces) beans of your choice, drained
- 1 small onion, chopped
- 1 can (15 ounces each) fire roasted tomatoes
- 1 medium red bell pepper, chopped
- ½ tablespoon chili powder or to taste
- Salt to taste
- ½ teaspoon garlic powder
- ½ teaspoon ground cumin
- Hot sauce to taste (optional)
- 2 teaspoons lime juice
- Sour cream and green onions to garnish

Method:

1. Add all the ingredients except lime juice, sour cream and green onions to the slow cooker.
2. Close the lid. Select 'Low' option and set the timer for 6-8 hours or on 'High' for 3 ½ hours.
3. Remove meat with a slotted spoon and place on your work area.
4. Shred with a pair of forks and add it back to the cooker. Stir well. Add lime juice and stir again.
5. Taste and adjust the seasonings if necessary.
6. Ladle into bowls.
7. Garnish with sour cream and green onions.

Chapter 9: Slow Cooker Side Dish Recipes

Spicy Black-Eyed Peas

Serves: 5

Ingredients:

- ½ pound dried black-eyed peas, sorted, rinsed
- 1 clove garlic, chopped
- 3 cups water
- 2 onions, chopped
- 1 small red bell peppers, deseeded, chopped
- ½ cube chicken bouillon
- 2 slices bacon, chopped
- 4 ounces ham, diced
- 1 jalapeño peppers, deseeded, minced
- ¼ teaspoon cayenne pepper
- Salt to taste
- Pepper to taste
- 1 teaspoon ground cumin

Method:

1. Add water and chicken bouillon cube into the slow cooker. It will dissolve in a few minutes.
2. Add rest of the ingredients to the slow cooker. Stir well.
3. Close the lid. Select 'Low' option and set the timer for 6-8 hours or on 'High' for 3 ½ hours or until beans are cooked.
4. Stir in between a couple of times while it is cooking.
5. Serve hot.

Loaded Baked Potato

Serves: 8

Ingredients:

- 8 medium russet potatoes, rinsed
- 1 medium head broccoli, cut into small florets, peel the stalks and chop into ½ inch pieces
- 20 ounces crimini mushrooms, trimmed, quartered
- 2 tablespoons chives, chopped
- ½ -1 cup hot vegetable or chicken broth
- 4 tablespoons sour cream or yogurt
- ¼ cup olive oil
- Salt to taste
- Pepper powder to taste

Method:

1. Take 8 sheets of foil and place a potato on each foil. Wrap the potatoes and place in the slow cooker.
2. Close the lid. Select 'Low' option and set the timer for 6-8 hours or on 'High' for 3 ½ hours or until potatoes are cooked.
3. Meanwhile, place a skillet over medium high heat. Add oil. When the oil is heated, add broccoli, salt and pepper and sauté until the broccoli is crisp as well as tender.
4. Remove the potatoes from the pot and cool. When cool enough to handle, halve the potatoes with a fork.
5. Scoop out the middle part of the potato and transfer into a bowl. Set aside the cases.
6. Add broth and yogurt or sour cream and mix well. Add salt and pepper and stir again.
7. Stuff this mixture in the potato cases.
8. Top the potatoes with the broccoli and serve warm.

German Potato Salad

Serves: 4

Ingredients:

- 1 pound russet potatoes, peeled, cut into ¼ inch thick slices
- 1 large onion, chopped
- ½ cup celery, chopped
- A handful fresh parsley, chopped
- 4 slices bacon
- 1 tablespoon quick cooking tapioca
- 1/3 cup apple cider vinegar
- 2 tablespoons raw sugar
- Salt to taste
- Pepper to taste
- ½ cup water

Method:

1. Add onion, potato and celery to the slow cooker.
2. Mix together in a bowl, water, vinegar, sugar, tapioca, salt and pepper and add to the cooker over the potatoes.
3. Close the lid. Select 'Low' option and set the timer for 6-8 hours or on 'High' for 3 ½ hours or until potatoes are cooked.
4. Meanwhile, place a skillet over medium heat. Add bacon and cook until crisp. Remove with a slotted spoon and place over paper towels.
5. When cool enough to handle, crumble the bacon and set aside.
6. Remove the potatoes from the pot and cool for 5-8 minutes.
7. Transfer into a serving bowl.
8. Add bacon and parsley and mix well.

Refried Beans

Serves: 6-8

Ingredients:

- 1 ½ cups dried pinto beans, rinsed
- 1 tablespoon garlic, minced
- 1 small onion, quartered
- 2-3 teaspoons salt
- Pepper to taste
- 5 cups water
- ¼ teaspoon ground cumin
- ½ fresh jalapeno pepper, sliced
- Cheddar cheese to serve

Method:

1. Add all the ingredients to the slow cooker.
2. Add rest of the ingredients to the slow cooker. Stir well.
3. Close the lid. Select 'Low' option and set the timer for 8-9 hours or on 'High' for 4 hours or until beans are cooked.
4. Stir in between a couple of times while it is cooking.
5. Drain and retain some of the cooked liquid.
6. Add the ingredients into a blender and blend to the consistency you desire adding the retained liquid.
7. Garnish with cheese and serve.

Baked Potatoes

Serves: 8

Ingredients:

- 8 potatoes, scrubbed, rinsed
- Salt to taste
- 2 tablespoons extra virgin olive oil
- 8 sheets aluminum foil

Method:

1. Take 8 sheets of aluminum foil.
2. Prick each of the potatoes all over with a fork. Rub oil all over it. Season with salt and place each on a foil.
3. Wrap it tightly and place in the slow cooker.
4. Close the lid. Select 'Low' option and set the timer for 6-8 hours or on 'High' for 3 ½ hours or until potatoes are cooked.
5. Remove from the pot and cool for a while. Unwrap and serve.

Texas Style Baked Beans

Serves: 6

Ingredients:

- ½ pound ground beef
- 1 small onion, chopped
- 2 cans (16 ounces each) baked beans with pork
- ½ cup barbeque sauce
- ½ tablespoon chili powder
- 2 ounces canned chopped green chili pepper
- ¼ cup brown sugar
- 4 teaspoons hot pepper sauce or to taste
- 1 ½ teaspoons garlic powder
- Salt to taste

Method:

1. Place a skillet over medium heat. Add beef and sauté until it is brown. Drain the excess fat and place beef in the slow cooker.
2. Add rest of the ingredients and stir.
3. Close the lid. Select 'Low' option and set the timer for 4 hours or on 'High' for 2 hours.
4. Stir in between a couple of times while it is cooking.
5. Serve hot.

Bavarian Red Cabbage

Serves: 3

Ingredients:

- 1 medium head red cabbage, rinsed, sliced
- 3 tart apples, cored, quartered
- 1 cup hot water
- 1/3 cup apple cider vinegar
- 1 medium onion, chopped
- 1 teaspoon salt
- 2 teaspoons sugar
- 3 tablespoons butter or bacon fat

Method:

1. Add all the ingredients into the slow cooker. Stir well.
2. Close the lid. Select 'Low' option and set the timer for 3-4 hours or on 'High' for1 ½ - 2 hours.
3. Stir in between a couple of times while it is cooking.
4. Serve hot.

Chicken Taco Salad

Serves: 8

Ingredients:

- 1 ¾ pounds chicken breast, skinless, boneless
- 8 cups iceberg lettuce, shredded
- 3 small whole tomatoes, quartered
- 2 ½ cups chunky salsa
- 12 ounces button mushrooms, sliced
- 4 tablespoons taco seasoning
- 1 ½ cups frozen peas
- 1 ½ cups black beans
- 2 ½ cups cheddar cheese, finely shredded
- Salt to taste
- Tortilla chips to serve (optional)

Method:

1. Add chicken, taco seasoning and salsa into the slow cooker and stir.
2. Close the lid. Select 'Low' option and set the timer for 4-5 hours or on 'High' for 2-3 hours until the chicken is tender.
3. Remove the chicken with a slotted spoon. Place on your cutting board. When cool enough to handle, chop into small pieces.
4. Add rest of the ingredients except chicken and tortilla chips to a bowl and toss well.
5. Place cooked chicken over the salad and serve with tortilla chips.

Chapter 10: Slow Cooker Main Course Recipes

Citrus Chicken

Serves: 2-3

Ingredients:

- 1 pound bone- -in chicken thighs and legs
- Juice of an orange, retain the orange halves
- Juice of a lime, retain the lime halves
- Juice of a lemon, retain the lemon halves
- 1 small onion, quartered
- 2 cloves garlic, peeled, smashed
- Salt to taste

Method:

1. Place chicken in the slow cooker. Sprinkle some salt over it.
2. Add a little salt, orange juice, lemon juice and lime juice into a bowl and mix well.
3. Retain ¼ of the juice mixture and pour the rest on the chicken.
4. Add onion, garlic, orange and lemon and lime halves.
5. Close the lid. Select 'Low' option and set the timer for 5-6 hours or on 'High' for 3-4 hours or until the chicken is tender and coming off the bone.
6. Discard the citrus halves.
7. Remove the chicken and place on a baking sheet. Pour about 4 teaspoons of the liquid in the cooker on the chicken.
8. Broil until the skin of the chicken is crisp.
9. Serve with the liquid that is remaining in the cooker (add the liquid into a bowl and dip the chicken in it and enjoy).

Easy Cheesy Chicken Rice and Broccoli

Serves: 4

Ingredients:

- 1 ½ cups brown rice, rinsed
- 1 can fat free broccoli cheese soup
- 8 ounces frozen broccoli
- ½ cup cheddar cheese, shredded
- 3 cups water
- 3 frozen chicken breasts, skinless, boneless, thawed
- Salt to taste
- Pepper powder to taste
- Seasoning of your choice, to taste

Method:

1. Add rice, half can soup, water, and broccoli to the slow cooker.
2. Place the chicken over the rice. Pour the remaining soup on the chicken. Sprinkle salt, pepper and seasonings.
3. Close the lid. Select 'Low' option and set the timer for 6 hours or on 'High' for 3 hours or until the chicken is tender.
4. Sprinkle cheese on top and keep covered for a few minutes until the cheese melts.
5. Serve chicken over the rice.

Fajita Salsa Chicken

Serves: 6-8

Ingredients:

- 3 pounds chicken breast or thighs, skinless
- 1 red bell pepper, thinly sliced
- 1 green bell pepper, thinly sliced
- 1 yellow bell pepper, thinly sliced
- 1 orange bell pepper, thinly sliced
- 1 ½ jars (16 ounces each) salsa
- 2 tablespoons taco seasoning mix or to taste
- 3 tablespoons lemon juice
- Salt to taste
- Cooking spray

Method:

1. Spray the inside of the slow cooker with cooking spray.
2. Season the chicken breasts with taco seasoning. Place the chicken in the cooker.
3. Pour about ¾ of the salsa over the chicken.
4. Close the lid. Select 'Low' option and set the timer for 6 hours or on 'High' for 3 hours or until the chicken is tender.
5. Remove the chicken with a slotted spoon and place on your cutting board.
6. When cool enough to handle, shred with a pair of forks.
7. Add it back to the pot. Add remaining salsa and lemon juice and stir.
8. Taste and adjust the seasoning and salsa if necessary.
9. Pour salsa over the chicken and serve hot.

Garlicky Chicken

Serves: 3

Ingredients:

- 1 ½ pounds chicken
- 8 cloves garlic, minced
- ½ teaspoon garlic powder
- ¼ cup fresh parsley, chopped
- 1/3 cup lemon juice
- 6 tablespoons olive oil
- ½ teaspoon pepper powder
- ½ teaspoon salt or to taste

Method:

1. Add all the ingredients into the slow cooker. Mix well.
2. Close the lid. Select 'Low' option and set the timer for 4-6 hours or on 'High' for 2 - 3 hours.
3. Serve on a bed of shredded cabbage.

Creamy Mushroom Chicken

Serves: 6

Ingredients:

- 2 ½ pounds chicken tenderloins or sliced chicken breasts
- 1 pound baby portabella mushrooms
- Salt to taste
- Pepper to taste
- 2 cans cream of chicken soup

Method:

1. Place the chicken at the bottom of the slow cooker. Place the mushrooms over it.
2. Pour soup all over the mushrooms. Season with salt and pepper.
3. Close the lid. Select 'Low' option and set the timer for 4-5 hours or on 'High' for 2-3 hours or until the chicken is tender.
4. Stir and serve.

Baked Chicken with Summer Vegetables

Serves: 4

Ingredients:

- 1 ½ pounds chicken
- 1 tablespoon Dijon mustard
- ½ teaspoon dried thyme
- 2 large cloves garlic, minced
- 1 bell pepper, sliced
- ¼ cup white wine
- Salt to taste
- Pepper to taste
- 1 medium, cut into thick wedges
- 1 small green bell pepper, sliced
- 1 small red bell pepper, sliced
- 1 large tomato, chopped
- Cooking spray

Method:

1. Spray the inside of the slow cooker with cooking spray.
2. Rub the chicken with Dijon mustard. Sprinkle salt, pepper and thyme over it.
3. Place the chicken in the cooker.
4. Layer with the vegetables. Pour wine on top.
5. Close the lid. Select 'Low' option and set the timer for 4-5 hours or on 'High' for 2-3 hours or until the chicken is tender.
6. Serve with baked potatoes or with pasta.

Zesty Chicken with Couscous

Serves: 4-6

Ingredients:

- 1 whole chicken (2-3 pounds), cleaned
- 2 teaspoons salt
- ½ teaspoon cayenne pepper
- 1 teaspoon paprika
- 1 ½ teaspoons onion powder
- ½ teaspoon white pepper
- ½ teaspoon black pepper
- 1 teaspoon dried thyme
- 2 large onions, thinly sliced
- 1 teaspoon garlic powder or 4 cloves garlic, minced
- 1 ½ boxes couscous

Method:

1. Remove the giblets from the chicken and use it in some other recipe.
2. Spread the onions at the bottom of the slow cooker.
3. Add all the spices in a bowl and mix well. Rub this mixture all over the chicken and place over the onions.
4. Close the lid. Select 'Low' option and set the timer for 7-9 hours or on 'High' for 5-6 hours or until the chicken is tender.
5. When done, drain the cooked liquid into a saucepan.
6. Add couscous into the saucepan and stir. Let it sit for 5 minutes.
7. Serve chicken with couscous.

Chicken N Beans

Serves: 6-8

Ingredients:

- 2 pounds chicken, uncooked
- 3 cups canned or cooked black beans
- 3 cups canned or cooked garbanzo beans
- 3 cups corn kernels
- 1 cup salsa Verde
- 2 cups homemade salsa
- ½ cup cilantro, chopped

Method:

1. Add all the ingredients except half the cilantro into a slow cooker. Mix well.
2. Close the lid. Select 'Low' option and set the timer for 6-7 hours or on 'High' for 3 hours.
3. When done, stir in the cilantro.
4. Serve over hot steamed rice or warmed corn tortillas or with corn bread.

Buffalo Chicken Lettuce Wraps

Serves: 3

Ingredients:

For the chicken:

- 12 ounces chicken breast, skinless, boneless
- 1 small onion, chopped
- 8 ounces low sodium chicken broth
- 1 small celery stalk
- 1 clove garlic, minced
- ¼ cup hot cayenne pepper sauce

For the wraps:

- 3 large lettuce leaves
- 1 large stalk celery, cut into 2 inch matchsticks
- 1 medium carrot, shredded
- Dressing of your choice

Method:

1. Add all the ingredients of the chicken except hot sauce into the slow cooker and stir.
2. Close the lid. Select 'Low' option and set the timer for 7-8 hours or on 'High' for 3-4 hours.
3. Remove the chicken with a slotted spoon and place on your work area.
4. When cool enough to handle, shred with a pair of forks. Add it back into the cooker.
5. Add hot sauce and stir.
6. Place the lettuce leaves on your work area. Divide the chicken among the lettuce leaves.
7. Place some carrots and celery. Add a dollop of dressing. Wrap and serve.

Cauliflower Rice Greek Chicken Bowl

Serves: 6-8

Ingredients:

For chicken:

- 6 large chicken breasts, trimmed, cut into strips lengthwise
- 1 ½ tablespoons Greek seasoning
- 1 teaspoon Greek oregano
- 3 tablespoons extra virgin olive oil
- Juice of 1 ½ lemons
- 1 ½ teaspoons lemon zest, grated
- Freshly ground pepper to taste
- Cooking spray

For cauliflower rice:

- 2 medium heads cauliflower, grated to rice like consistency
- 1 large onion, finely chopped
- 2 teaspoons Greek seasoning
- 2 medium green bell peppers, finely chopped
- 1 ½ tablespoons extra virgin olive oil
- Salt to taste
- Freshly ground pepper to taste

For Greek salsa:

- 4-5 medium cucumbers, chopped
- 1/3 cup kalamata olives or black olives, chopped
- ¾ cup feta cheese, crumbled
- 1 ½ cups cherry tomatoes, chopped
- 1/3 cup red onion, finely chopped
- 1/3 cup or more low carb Italian dressing of your choice

Method:

1. To make chicken: Add lemon juice, zest, Greek seasoning, oil, oregano and black pepper into a bowl and stir.
2. Spray the inside of the slow cooker with cooking spray. Place chicken in the slow cooker. Pour the lemon juice mixture over it.
3. Close the lid. Select 'Low' option and set the timer for 6-7 hours or on 'High' for 3-4 hours.
4. When done, remove the chicken with a slotted spoon and place on your cutting board. Shred with a pair of forks. Add it back into the pot and stir. Keep warm.
5. To make Greek salsa: Add all the ingredients of Greek salsa into a bowl. Cover and refrigerate until use.
6. To make cauliflower rice: You can add cauliflower florets into a food processor and pulse until you get a rice like texture. Alternately, you can grate with a grater.
7. Place a wok or large skillet over medium high heat. Add oil. When the oil is heated, add onions and bell peppers and sauté until slightly soft.
8. Add Greek seasoning and sauté for a few seconds until fragrant.
9. Add cauliflower rice and sauté for 3-4 minutes until crisp as well as tender. Add salt and pepper and stir. Remove from heat.
10. To serve: Divide the cauliflower rice among individual serving bowls. Divide the chicken and place over the cauliflower rice. Top with Greek salsa.
11. Serve immediately.

Turkey Shepherd's Pie

Serves: 8

Ingredients:

- 24 ounces turkey, chopped into strips or cubes
- 2 jars (12 ounces each) chicken or turkey gravy
- 20 ounces loose pack frozen mixed vegetables
- 1 cup frozen corn kernels, thawed
- 2 packages (20 ounces each) refrigerated mashed potatoes
- 2 teaspoons dried thyme crushed
- Salt to taste
- Pepper to taste
- Cooking spray

Method:

1. Grease the inside of the slow cooker with cooking spray.
2. Place turkey in the pot. Pour gravy over it. Sprinkle thyme over it.
3. Close the lid. Select 'Low' option and set the timer for 6-7 hours or on 'High' for 3-4 hours or until the turkey is tender.
4. Layer with vegetables followed by corn and finally mashed potatoes. Sprinkle salt and pepper.
5. Close the lid. Select 'Low' and set the timer for 1 hour or on 'High' for 30 minutes.

Sesame Ginger Turkey Wraps

Serves: 4-8

Ingredients:

- 2 turkey thighs, skinless
- 3 tablespoons water
- 8 whole wheat tortilla (8 inches each)
- 2/3 cup sesame ginger stir fry sauce
- 12 ounces shredded broccoli slaw mix
- 4 green onions, sliced
- Cooking spray

Method:

1. Grease the inside of the slow cooker with cooking spray.
2. Place turkey in the slow cooker.
3. Add water and sesame ginger stir-fry sauce in a bowl and mix.
4. Close the lid. Select 'Low' option and set the timer for 6-7 hours or on 'High' for 3-4 hours or until the turkey is tender.
5. Remove the turkey with a slotted spoon and place on your work area.
6. When cool enough to handle, shred the turkey with a pair of forks. Discard the bones.
7. Add the shredded turkey back into the cooker and stir.
8. Add broccoli mixture and stir.
9. Cover and let it sit for 5 minutes.
10. Warm the tortillas according to the instructions on the package.
11. Place the shredded turkey on each of the tortillas. Sprinkle green onions. Drizzle some of the cooked juice.
12. Roll and serve.

Pad Thai

Serves: 2

Ingredients:

- 1 cup leftover turkey, cubed
- ¼ cup hot water
- 1 tablespoon rice vinegar
- ½ tablespoon chili garlic sauce
- 2 scallions, chopped
- 1 small onion, sliced
- ½ cup Napa cabbage, chopped, packed
- ½ cup Bok Choy, chopped, packed
- 1 cup broccoli slaw, packed
- 2 tablespoons raw sugar
- 1 tablespoon low sodium soy sauce
- 2 tablespoons lime juice
- ¼ cup fresh cilantro, chopped
- 2 cloves garlic, minced
- Salt to taste
- 4 ounce whole wheat linguine, cook according to instructions on the package

Method:

1. Add water, sugar, vinegar, and chili garlic sauce and lime juice into a bowl and stir until the sugar is dissolved.
2. Add turkey into the slow cooker and cover the turkey with the sauce mixture. Add rest of the ingredients except linguine and mix well.
3. Close the lid. Select 'Low' option and set the timer for 6 hours or on 'High' for 3 hours.
4. When done, add linguini into the cooker. Toss well and serve.

Gingered Beef

Serves: 3

Ingredients:

- ¾ pound beef round steak, boneless, cut into 1 inch cubes
- 2 scallions, sliced
- 2 medium carrots, sliced into ½ inch thick slices
- 1 clove garlic, minced
- 1 small red bell pepper, chopped
- 1 cup frozen sugar snap peas, frozen, thawed
- 1 medium onion, sliced
- 2 teaspoons fresh ginger, grated
- 1 tablespoon low sodium soy sauce
- 1 teaspoon instant beef bouillon granules
- 1 ½ tablespoons cornstarch mixed with 2 tablespoons water
- 1 cup water
- Cooked rice to serve

Method:

1. Add all the ingredients except the rice; the cornstarch mixture and sugar snap peas into the slow cooker. Mix well.
2. Close the lid. Select 'Low' option and set the timer for 9-10 hours or on 'High' for 4-5 hours.
3. Add cornstarch mixture after about 8 ½ hours of cooking. Stir a couple of times.
4. During the last 10 minutes of cooking, add sugar snap peas and mix well.
5. Serve over hot rice.

Korean Beef

Serves: 4

Ingredients:

- 1 ½ pounds boneless chuck roast, cubed
- 2 cloves garlic, minced
- ½ cup beef broth
- ½ tablespoon ginger, minced or grated
- 2 teaspoons sesame oil
- Sriracha sauce to taste
- ½ tablespoon rice wine vinegar
- Salt to taste
- White pepper to taste
- 1 tablespoon cornstarch mixed with a bit of water
- ½ teaspoon onion powder
- ¼ cup brown sugar, packed
- ¼ cup low sodium soy sauce
- 1 teaspoon sesame seeds
- 1 green onion, thinly sliced
-

Method:

1. Add broth, soy sauce, salt, brown sugar, garlic, ginger, oil, vinegar, Sriracha, onion powder and white pepper into a bowl and stir until well combined.
2. Add chuck and the mixture into the slow cooker. Stir.
3. Close the lid. Select 'Low' option and set the timer for 7-8 hours or on 'High' for 3-4 hours.
4. Add cornstarch mixture and stir. Cook on 'High' for 30 minutes or until the sauce thickens.
5. Garnish with green onions and sesame seeds and serve.

Beef Shawarma

Serves: 3-4

Ingredients:

- 3 tablespoons lemon juice
- ½ teaspoon salt
- Red pepper to taste
- 1 ½ pounds thin cut beef steak, boneless
- ½ small cucumber, chopped
- 3 tablespoons olive oil
- 1 teaspoon curry powder or to taste
- 2 cloves garlic, crushed
- ½ cup plain yogurt or Greek yogurt
- Salt to taste
- Pepper to taste
- Pita bread to serve

Method:

1. Add lemon juice, oil, cayenne pepper, curry powder and garlic into a bowl and mix.
2. Place beefsteak in the slow cooker. Pour the oil mixture over the beef. Stir.
3. Close the lid. Select 'Low' option and set the timer for 7 -8 hours or on 'High' for 5-6 hours or until the meat is tender.
4. Mix together in a bowl, cucumber and yogurt. Add salt and pepper and stir.
5. Serve beef in pita bread with the cucumber yogurt sauce.

Corned Beef Brisket

Serves: 4

Ingredients:

- 2 pounds corned beef brisket with spice packet, trimmed of fat,
- 1 small onion, quartered
- ¼ small head cabbage, chopped into 2 wedges
- 1 medium yellow potato, cut into 2 inch pieces
- 2 medium carrots, peeled, cut into 2 inch pieces
- ¼ cup water
- Salt to taste

Method:

1. Rub the contents of the spice packet all over the beef.
2. Place all the vegetables in the slow cooker. Pour water over it. Place beef over the vegetables.
3. Close the lid. Select 'Low' option and set the timer for 9-12 hours or on 'High' for 5-6 hours.
4. Remove the beef and place on your cutting board. When cool enough to handle, slice the beef against the grain and serve with the cooked vegetables.

African Pulled Beef Sandwiches with Yogurt Mint Sauce

Serves: 4-5

Ingredients:

- 1 ½ pounds chuck roast
- ½ teaspoon ground cumin
- ¼ teaspoon ground allspice
- 1 small jalapeño, deseeded, diced
- 3 whole cloves garlic, peeled,
- ¼ teaspoon ground red pepper or cayenne pepper
- 1 onion, chopped
- 7.5 ounces canned diced tomatoes or use equivalent amount of fresh tomatoes

For yogurt mint sauce:

- ½ cup Greek yogurt
- ¼ teaspoon dried mint
- 1 medium cucumber, finely chopped
- ¼ teaspoon dried mint or 1 teaspoon fresh mint leaves, minced

Method:

1. Retain one clove of garlic and crush the other 2.
2. Halve the whole garlic and rub it all over the roast.
3. Place the roast, crushed garlic and halved garlic in the slow cooker. Sprinkle cumin, red pepper and allspice over it.
4. Close the lid. Select 'Low' option and set the timer for 7-8 hours or on 'High' for 5-6 hours or until the meat is tender.
5. Remove the turkey with a slotted spoon and place on your cutting board.
6. When cool enough to handle, shred with a pair of forks.
7. Add it back to the pot. Mix well.
8. Meanwhile, make the yogurt mint sauce as follows: Mix together all the ingredients of the yogurt mint sauce.
9. Cover and refrigerate until use.

Cinnamon Pot Roast

Serves: 4

Ingredients:

- 1 ½ pounds chuck roast, trimmed of excess fat
- 1 large onion, chopped
- 14 ounces diced tomatoes
- A handful fresh parsley or mint
- 1 teaspoon garlic, minced
- 1 tablespoon oil
- 2 cinnamon sticks
- 1 teaspoon pepper powder or to taste
- 1 teaspoon salt or to taste

Method:

1. Sprinkle salt and pepper over the roast.
2. Place a large skillet over medium heat. Add onions and garlic. Sauté until the onions are translucent.
3. Add the roast and cook on both the sides until brown. Transfer into the slow cooker.
4. Add rest of the ingredients and mix well.
5. Close the lid. Select 'Low' option and set the timer for 7-8 hours or on 'High' for 5-6 hours or until the meat is tender.
6. Remove the meat from the cooker and place on your cutting board.
7. When cool enough to handle, slice the meat against the grain
8. Pour the sauce over the roast and serve hot garnished with mint or parsley.

Asian Short Ribs

Serves: 6-8

Ingredients:

- 6 pounds short ribs, cut into 2-3 inch pieces, trimmed of fat
- 1 teaspoon canola oil
- 1 ½ tablespoons apricot fruit spread
- 2 teaspoons rice wine vinegar
- 3 cloves garlic, minced
- 2 green onions, thinly sliced
- ½ teaspoon sea salt
- 2 tablespoons soy sauce
- 1 ½ tablespoons tomato paste
- 2 teaspoons fresh ginger, minced
- 2 teaspoons sesame seeds, toasted
- ¼ teaspoon five spice powder

Method:

1. Season the ribs with salt.
2. Place a large skillet over medium heat.
3. Add the ribs and cook on all the sides until brown. Transfer into the slow cooker.
4. Add rest of the ingredients into a bowl. Add 2 tablespoons water and mix well. Pour over the ribs.
5. Close the lid. Select 'Low' option and set the timer for 7-8 hours or on 'High' for 5-6 hours or until the meat is tender.
6. Remove the ribs with a slotted spoon and place on a plate. Cover with foil and set aside.
7. Transfer the cooked liquid in a glass and let it sit for a while. Discard the fat that will float on the top.
8. Pour the liquid in the ribs and serve garnished with green onions and sesame seeds.

Italian Zucchini Meat loaf

Serves: 12-14

Ingredients:

For meatloaf:

- 3 pounds ground beef or bison
- 3 tablespoons onion powder
- 6 cloves garlic crushed
- 1 ½ cups zucchini, shredded, squeezed of moisture
- ¾ cup Italian parsley, finely chopped
- 3 large eggs, beaten
- 4 ½ tablespoons balsamic vinegar
- ¾ cup parmesan cheese
- 2 tablespoons dried oregano
- ½ teaspoon pepper or to taste
- Cooking spray

For topping:

- 1/3 cup ketchup
- 4 tablespoons Italian parsley, chopped
- 1/3 cup low fat mozzarella cheese, shredded

Method:

1. Mix together all the ingredients of the meatloaf with your hands.
2. Line the bottom of the slow cooker with 2 double folded sheets of aluminum foil in a crisscross manner. Spray with cooking spray.
3. Using your hands, shape the dough into a loaf and place it in the slow cooker.
4. Close the lid. Select 'Low' option and set the timer for 6 hours or on 'High' for 3 hours.
5. Brush with ketchup. Sprinkle cheese on it.
6. Cook for a few minutes until cheese melts.
7. Garnish with parsley.
8. Slice and serve with whole-wheat pasta.

Lamb with Olives and Potatoes

Serves: 4

Ingredients:

- 1 ¾ pounds lamb shanks
- ¾ pound small potatoes, halved
- 2 cloves garlic, minced
- 2 large shallots or onions, cut into wedges
- 1 teaspoon dried rosemary or 2 sprigs fresh rosemary
- 1 tablespoon lemon juice
- 1 teaspoon lemon zest, grated
- ½ cup chicken broth
- 2-3 tablespoons whole wheat flour
- ¼ cup dry wine
- Salt to taste
- Pepper to taste
- A handful fresh parsley, chopped
- 1 tablespoon extra virgin olive oil
- ½ cup green olives, pitted, halved

Method:

1. Add potatoes, shallots, lemon zest, garlic and rosemary into the slow cooker. Stir.
2. Add about a tablespoon of flour to broth. Whisk well and pour into the slow cooker.
3. Place remaining flour on a plate. Sprinkle salt and pepper over the flour and dredge in the flour. Shake to remove excess flour.
4. Place a large skillet over medium high heat with oil. Add lamb shanks and cook until brown on all sides. Transfer into the slow cooker. Cook in batches if required.
5. Add wine into the skillet and scrape the bottom of the skillet to remove any browned bits that are stuck. Simmer until it is reduced to half its original quantity. Pour the wine into the slow cooker.
6. Close the lid. Select 'Low' option and set the timer for 7-8 hours or on 'High' for 3 ½ -4 hours or until the meat is tender. Add olives and stir. Cook for 15-20 minutes.
7. Serve lamb with potatoes.

Smoky Spicy Lamb Roast

Serves: 2

Ingredients:

- 2 large lamb chops
- 1 onion, sliced into rings
- 1 can (8 ounce diced green chilies
- 1 can (14.5 ounce each) fire roasted diced tomatoes
- 1 small red and yellow bell pepper, diced
- ½ teaspoon cumin powder
- ½ teaspoon paprika
- Salt to taste
- ½ teaspoon coriander powder
- Pepper powder to taste
- ½ teaspoon chili powder or to taste
- ½ teaspoon garlic powder

Method:

1. Add all the ingredients to the slow cooker. Mix well.
2. Close the lid. Select 'Low' option and set the timer for 6-8 hours or on 'High' for 3 ½ -4 hours or until the meat is tender.
3. Serve lamb with the vegetables.

Moroccan Lamb Shank

Serves: 1

Ingredients:

- 1 whole lamb shank, trimmed of fat
- 1 medium onion, chopped
- 2 cloves garlic, minced
- 1 small red bell pepper, chopped
- 7 ounces canned diced tomatoes
- ¼ cup whole olives, drained
- ½ cup canned or cooked garbanzo beans, rinsed, drained
- ½ lemon, unpeeled, chopped into pieces
- ½ teaspoon raw sugar
- ½ teaspoon ground coriander
- ½ teaspoon ground cumin
- Salt to taste
- Pepper to taste
- ¾ cup water
- 1 teaspoon olive oil
- 1 stick cinnamon (about 2 inches)
- 2 tablespoons golden raisins

Method:

1. Add lemon, sugar and salt into a bowl and stir. Set aside for a while.
2. Season the lamb shank with salt and pepper.
3. Place a skillet over medium heat. Add oil. When the oil is heated, add lamb shank and cook until brown on all the sides. Remove from the pan and set aside.
4. Place the pan back on heat. Add onions, bell pepper and garlic. Sauté for a couple of minutes and transfer into the slow cooker.
5. Add rest of the ingredients except raisins and mix well. Add lamb and stir. Cover the lamb with the mixture in the pot.
6. Close the lid. Select 'Low' option and set the timer for 8-9 hours or on 'High' for 4-5 hours.
7. Add raisins after about 4 hours of cooking. Also add the lemon mixture to it. Mix well and cover again.
8. When done, discard cinnamon and the lemon pieces and serve.

Mexican Style Shredded Pork

Serves: 6 -8

Ingredients:

- 4 ½ pounds pork loin roast, boneless, cut into 2 inch pieces
- 3 cans (4 ounces each) diced green chili peppers
- 1/3 cup chipotle sauce
- 2 ¼ cups long grain brown rice
- 4 ½ cups water, divided
- 1/3 cup fresh lime juice
- 1 teaspoon salt
- 5 cloves garlic, crushed
- 1/3 cup fresh cilantro, chopped

Method:

1. Sprinkle salt over the roast and place in the slow cooker.
2. Pour chili pepper, chipotle sauce and 2/3 cup water on it. Sprinkle garlic.
3. Close the lid. Select 'Low' option and set the timer for 7 hours or on 'High' for 3 ½ hours.
4. Meanwhile, cook rice in a saucepan (cover with a lid) with remaining water. When the rice is nearly cooked, add lime juice and cilantro and stir. Keep warm.
5. When the roast is cooked, remove with a slotted spoon and place on your work area. When cool enough to handle, shred with a pair of forks.
6. Add it back into the cooker and stir. Let it sit for a while.
7. Serve over cooked brown rice.

Carnitas Tacos

Serves: 10-12

Ingredients:

- 3 pounds pork shoulder or pork loin roast
- 1 ½ teaspoons ground cumin
- 2 teaspoons taco seasoning or to taste
- 1 ½ teaspoons mild chili powder
- Salt to taste
- 1 ½ teaspoons garlic powder
- 1/3 cup fresh orange juice
- 3 tablespoons lemon juice

For the tacos (optional): Use any

- 10-12 tortillas, warmed according to the instructions on the package
- Queso fresco
- Lime wedges
- Sour cream to serve
- Cheddar cheese, shredded
- Avocado slices
- Thinly sliced cabbage
- Salsa

Method:

1. Add taco seasoning, salt, chili powder, and garlic powder and ground cumin into a bowl and stir. Season pork with taco seasoning mixture.
2. Place the roast in the slow cooker.
3. Mix together lemon juice and orange juice and pour over it.
4. Close the lid. Select 'Low' option and set the timer for 8-9 hours or on 'High' for 4-5 hours or until the pork is tender.
5. Remove the pork with a slotted spoon. Shred with a pair of forks and add it back to the pot. Mix well.
6. Transfer on to a baking sheet that is lined with foil.
7. Broil in the oven for 10-15 minutes until pork begins to turn crisp.
8. Place about ½ cup pork on each tortilla. Add the toppings you are using.
9. Roll and serve.

White Beans with Aji Verde Sauce

Serves: 6

Ingredients:

- ½ pound dry northern beans or navy beans, soaked in water overnight, drained
- 1 small onion, chopped
- 1 small onion, quartered
- 2 ounces ham hock
- ½ green bell pepper, chopped
- 1 chicken bouillon cube
- 1 bay leaf
- 1 large clove garlic, minced
- ¼ teaspoon Goya adobo or to taste
- ¼ cup fresh cilantro, chopped
- ½ teaspoon ground cumin
- Salt to taste
- 4 cups water

For Aji Verde sauce:

- 5-6 jalapeños, deseeded
- 2 tablespoons olive oil
- 2 tablespoons fresh cilantro
- 2 tablespoons white vinegar
- 2 cloves garlic, peeled
- 2 tablespoons fat free sour cream
- ¼ teaspoon ground cumin
- Pepper to taste
- Salt to taste

Method:

1. Place a skillet over medium heat. Add oil. When the oil is heated, add chopped onion and garlic and sauté for a few minutes until the onions are translucent.
2. Add cilantro and salt and sauté for a minute. Transfer into the slow cooker.
3. Add beans, water, quartered onion, ham hock, green pepper and bay leaf into the cooker.

4. Close the lid. Select 'Low' option and set the timer for 7-8 hours or on 'High' for 4-5 hours or until the beans are cooked.
5. Add chicken bouillon, cumin and adobo. Stir well.
6. Cover and cook on 'High' for 15 minutes.
7. Taste and adjust the seasonings if necessary. Discard the bay leaf and ham hock.
8. Meanwhile, make the aji Verde sauce as follows: Add all the ingredients of the sauce into a blender and blend until smooth.
9. Serve aji Verde sauce over the beans and with brown rice.

Italian Braised Pork

Serves: 3

Ingredients:

- 4 teaspoons olive oil
- 1 medium yellow onion, chopped
- 2 pounds boneless pork shoulder
- Salt to taste
- Pepper to taste
- 2 cloves garlic, minced
- ½ teaspoon fennel seeds
- 1 small stalk celery, chopped
- 20 ounces crushed tomatoes
- 1/3 cup dry red wine
- 3 cups cooked couscous to serve

Method:

1. Place a skillet over medium high heat. Sprinkle salt and pepper over the pork and place in the skillet. Cook until brown on all sides.
2. Place the pork in the slow cooker.
3. Place the pan back on heat and add garlic, onion, celery and fennel seeds. Sauté until the onions are translucent.
4. Add wine and scrape the bottom of the pan to remove any browned bits that are stuck. Simmer until the wine is reduced to half its original quantity. Transfer into the cooker.
5. Also add the tomatoes.
6. Close the lid. Select 'Low' option and set the timer for 8-9 hours or on 'High' for 4-5 hours or until the pork is tender.
7. Remove the pork with a slotted spoon. Shred with a pair of forks and add it back to the pot. Mix well.
8. Serve over couscous.

Ham Sandwiches

Serves: 12

Ingredients:

- 3 pounds bone-in ham
- ½ pound brown sugar
- 4 ounces yellow mustard
- 12 dinner rolls, split

Method:

1. Add ham into the slow cooker. Pour enough water to cover the ham.
2. Close the lid. Select 'Low' option and set the timer for 8-9 hours or on 'High' for 4-5 hours or until the pork is tender.
3. Remove the pork with a slotted spoon. Discard the water in the cooker. Shred with a pair of forks and add it back to the pot.
4. Add mustard and brown sugar and stir.
5. Close the lid. Select 'Low' and set the timer for 1 hour.
6. Serve over dinner rolls.

Sour Cream Pork Chops

Serves: 8

Ingredients:

- 8 pork chops
- 1 teaspoon garlic powder
- 2 medium onions, cut into ¼ inch thick slices
- 3 cups boiling water
- 3 cubes chicken bouillon
- 1 cup +3 tablespoons whole wheat flour
- Salt to taste
- Pepper to taste
- 10 ounces sour cream
- 2 teaspoons oil

Method:

1. Sprinkle salt, pepper and garlic powder over the pork chops.
2. Add 1-cup flour into a bowl and dredge the pork chop in it.
3. Place a skillet over medium heat. Add oil. When the oil is heated, add pork and cook until brown. Cook in batches.
4. Place in the slow cooker. Place onion on the chops.
5. Add bouillon cubes to boiling water and stir. Pour over the chops.
6. Close the lid. Select 'Low' option and set the timer for 8-9 hours or on 'High' for 4-5 hours or until the pork is tender.
7. Remove the pork with a slotted spoon and keep warm.
8. Mix remaining 3 tablespoons flour with a little water and add into the cooker.
9. Cook on 'High' for 15 minutes or until thick.
10. Place pork chops on a serving platter. Pour the sauce over it and serve.

Lemon Pepper Tilapia with Asparagus

Serves: 8

Ingredients:

- 8 tilapia fillets, thawed if frozen
- 1 bundle asparagus, chopped into 3-4 inch pieces
- 2 teaspoons lemon pepper seasoning or to taste
- 4 tablespoons butter
- 1 cup lemon juice

Method:

1. Take 8 sheets of foils. Lay the fillets in the middle of each foil. Sprinkle lemon pepper seasoning over it.
2. Place ½ tablespoon of butter on each of the fillets. Place asparagus over the fish.
3. Wrap foil all around the fish. Seal it well.
4. Place the packets in the slow cooker. It can be overlapped while placing it.
5. Close lid. Select 'Low' option and set the timer for 4 hours or on 'High' for 2 hours. Increase the cooking time if the fillets are not thawed.

Salmon Fillets and Asian-Style Vegetables

Serves: 4

Ingredients:

- 4 salmon fillets (5-6 ounces each)
- Salt to taste
- Pepper to taste
- 3 tablespoons honey
- 2 teaspoons sesame seeds (optional)
- 20-25 ounces frozen Asian stir fry vegetable blend
- 3 tablespoons lemon juice

Method:

1. Place the frozen vegetables to the bottom of the slow cooker.
2. Sprinkle salt and pepper over the fillets and place over the vegetable layer.
3. Add soy sauce, lemon juice and honey into a bowl and stir. Pour over the salmon and vegetables.
4. Sprinkle sesame seeds on it.
5. Close lid. Select 'Low' option and set the timer for 4 hours or on 'High' for 2 hours. Increase the cooking time if the fillets are not thawed.
6. Place over brown rice. Pour the sauce that is remaining in the cooker over the rice and serve.

Shrimp Scampi

Serves: 4-5

Ingredients:

- 2 pounds raw shrimp, peeled, deveined, thawed
- 4 tablespoons olive oil
- 1 cup white cooking wine
- 2 tablespoons garlic mined
- 2 tablespoons parsley, finely chopped
- Salt to taste
- Pepper powder to taste
- 1 teaspoon red pepper flakes

Method:

1. Add all the ingredients into the slow cooker and stir.
2. Close the lid. Select 'Low' option and set the timer for 2- 2 ½ hours or on 'High' for 1-½ hours. Increase the cooking time if the fillets are not thawed.
3. Stir and serve.

Shrimp N Spaghetti

Serves: 4

Ingredients:

- 1 ½ pounds shrimp, deveined, shelled
- 9 ounces tomato paste
- 24 ounces canned diced tomatoes
- 2 cloves garlic, minced
- Salt to taste
- Pepper to taste
- 1 teaspoon dried basil
- 1 teaspoon dried oregano
- 3 tablespoons parsley, minced
- ½ cup parmesan, cheese, or more to taste
- 1 teaspoon garlic salt or any other seasoned salt
- Cooked spaghetti to serve

Method:

1. Add all the ingredients except shrimp and cheese to the slow cooker.
2. Close the lid. Select 'Low' option and set the timer for 2- 2 ½ hours or on 'High' for 1-½ hours.
3. Add shrimp and stir.
4. Close the lid. Select 'High' and cook for 10-15 minutes.
5. Serve over spaghetti garnished with cheese.

Creamy Polenta with Chili Lime Shrimp

Serves: 8-12

Ingredients:

For polenta:

- 4 cups polenta or cornmeal
- 2 teaspoons salt or to taste
- 1 cup cheddar cheese, shredded
- 16 cups boiling water
- 2 cups frozen sweet corn kernels
- 1 cup parmesan cheese, shredded

For shrimp:

- 2 pounds small raw shrimp, peeled, deveined, tail off
- 4 tablespoons lime juice
- 4 cloves garlic, minced
- Pepper to taste
- Salt to taste
- ½ cup olive oil
- 2 teaspoons chili powder

Method:

1. Add cornmeal into the slow cooker. Pour boiling water over the cornmeal.
2. Add salt and corn and stir.
3. Close the lid. Select 'Low' option and set the timer for 6-7hours or on 'High' for 3-4 hours.
4. Add cheese and stir. Taste and add more salt if required. Cover and set aside for a while.
5. Meanwhile, make the shrimp as follows: Add all the ingredients of shrimp into a bowl. Stir well. Cover with a lid. Refrigerate for 10-15 minutes.
6. Place a skillet over medium high heat. Place shrimp in a single layer. Cook in batches.
7. Cook until the underside is brown. Flip sides and cook the other side too.
8. Ladle polenta into bowls. Place shrimp on top and serve.

Garlic Tilapia

Serves: 8

Ingredients:

- 8 tilapia fillets
- 2 teaspoons garlic, minced
- 4 tablespoons garlic butter, chopped into 8 small cubes
- 2 teaspoons parsley, minced
- Salt to taste
- Pepper powder to taste

Method:

1. Place foil at the bottom of pot. Lay the fillets in the middle of the slow cooker. Sprinkle salt and pepper over it.
2. Mix together in a bowl garlic and parsley.
3. Place a cube of butter on each of the fillet. Sprinkle the minced garlic and parsley mixture over the fillets.
4. Enclose the fillets in the foil. Seal it well.
5. Close the lid. Select 'Low' option and set the timer for 4-5 hours or on 'High' for 2 hours.

Healthy Shrimp Risotto

Ingredients:

- 4 ½ cups boiling water
- 1 ½ cups onions, chopped
- 1 ½ packages (9 ounce each) frozen artichoke hearts, thawed, quartered
- 1 tablespoon olive oil
- 2 tablespoons Better that Bouillon Lobster Base
- 5 cloves garlic, mined
- 1 ½ cups pearl barley
- 1 ½ pounds shrimp, peeled deveined
- 6 ounces baby spinach
- ½ cup parmesan cheese, grated
- 3 teaspoons lemon zest, grated
- Freshly ground black pepper to taste
- Salt to taste

Method:

1. Add lobster base to boiling water. Whisk well, set aside for a while.
2. Place a skillet over medium heat. Add oil and onions and sauté until onions are translucent.
3. Add garlic and sauté until fragrant. Transfer into the slow cooker.
4. Add lobster base solution and rest of the ingredients except spinach, lemon zest, cheese, and shrimp.
5. Close the lid. Select 'Low' option and set the timer for 4-5 hours or 'High' and set the timer for 2 ½ hours.
6. Add shrimp and cheese and stir.
7. Close lid. Cook on 'High' for 10-15 minutes.
8. Add lemon zest and baby spinach. Mix well.
9. Place in serving bowls and serve right away.

Refried Bean Tacos

Serves: 4

Ingredients:

For beans:

- 1 cups dried pinto beans, rinsed
- ½ -1 teaspoon salt
- 4 cups water

For toppings (optional): Use any

- 4 corn or whole wheat tortillas
- 2 green onions, thinly sliced
- 1-2 cups cabbage, red or green, thinly sliced
- 2 tomatoes, chopped
- ¼ teaspoon ground cumin
- ½ fresh jalapeno pepper, sliced
- Cheddar cheese
- Salsa
- Guacamole

Method:

1. Add all the ingredients of beans into the slow cooker.
2. Close the lid. Select 'Low' option and set the timer for 8-9 hours or 'High' and set the timer for 4 hours.
3. Drain the beans and retain some of the cooked liquid.
4. Blend the cooked ingredients to the consistency you desire adding the retained liquid.
5. Taste and adjust the salt if necessary.
6. Place the tortillas on your work area. Add the toppings, wrap and serve.

Healthy Enchiladas with Quinoa

Serves: 3-4

Ingredients:

- 1 small onion, finely chopped
- ½ teaspoon ground cumin
- ½ teaspoon mild chili powder (optional)
- 1 can (15 ounces) black beans, drained, rinsed
- 1 can (15 ounces) mild or medium red enchilada sauce, divided
- 7.5 ounces canned yellow corn, drained, rinsed
- 7.5 ounces canned diced fire roasted tomatoes with green chilies
- ½ cup quinoa, uncooked, rinsed
- ½ teaspoon salt
- ½ cup water
- 2 tablespoons lemon juice

For toppings (optional): Use any

- 1 cup cheddar cheese, shredded
- 2 tablespoons fresh cilantro, chopped
- 2 tablespoons sour cream
- 2 tomatoes, chopped
- 1 avocado, peeled, pitted, sliced
- Crushed corn chips
- Hot sauce
- Lime juice

Method:

1. Add all the ingredients into the slow cooker. Mix well.
2. Close the lid. Select 'Low' option and set the timer for 5-6 hours or 'High' for 2-3 hours.
3. Stir and serve with toppings of your choice.

Black Bean Stuffed Sweet Potatoes

Serves: 8-12

- 4 cans (15 ounces each) black beans, drained, rinsed
- 2 teaspoons garlic powder
- ½ teaspoon kosher salt
- 4 medium or 8 small sweet potatoes, scrubbed
- 3 cups salsa, divided
- 2 teaspoons smoked paprika
- 2/3 cup water

For toppings (optional): Use any

- 1 cup cheddar cheese, shredded
- 2 tablespoons fresh cilantro, chopped
- 2 tablespoons sour cream
- 2 tomatoes, chopped
- 1 avocado, peeled, pitted, sliced
- Crushed corn chips
- Hot sauce
- Lime juice
- 2 green onions, thinly sliced
- 1-2 cups cabbage, red or green, thinly sliced
- ¼ teaspoon ground cumin
- ½ fresh jalapeno pepper, sliced
- Cheddar cheese
- Salsa
- Guacamole
- Scallions

Method:

1. For sweet potatoes: Add beans, 2 cups salsa, garlic powder, water, smoked paprika and salt into the slow cooker and stir.
2. Place sweet potatoes on it.
3. Close the lid. Select 'Low' option and set the timer for 5-6 hours or 'High' for 2-3 hours.
4. Remove the sweet potatoes from the cooker and place on your cutting board.
5. When cool enough to handle, cut into 2 halves. Top with black beans and remaining salsa.
6. Serve with toppings of your choice.

Mushroom Stroganoff

Serves: 6

Ingredients:

- 2 pounds mushrooms, sliced
- 2 tablespoons butter
- 2 medium onions, halved, diced
- 5 cloves garlic, minced
- 4 cups hot vegetable stock
- 3 teaspoons smoked paprika
- 4 tablespoons ketchup
- Salt to taste
- Pepper powder to taste
- ½ cup sour cream
- ½ cup fresh parsley, chopped

Method:

1. Place a skillet over medium heat. Add butter. When butter melts, add onion and mushrooms and sauté until the mushrooms just begin to reduce in size.
2. Transfer the onions and mushrooms into the slow cooker.
3. Add all the ingredients except sour cream and parsley to the cooker.
4. Close the lid. Select 'Low' option and set the timer for 5-6 hours or 'High' for 2-3 hours.
5. Add sour cream and stir.
6. Sprinkle parsley and serve with whole wheat bread or whole-wheat pasta or brown rice.

Spring Veggie Coconut Curry

Serves:

Ingredients:

- ½ pound baby potatoes, quartered
- ½ pound asparagus, cut into 1 inch pieces
- ½ pound carrots, cut into 1 inch pieces
- ½ cup peas, thawed if frozen
- ¼ cup vegetable stock
- 1 cup canned or cooked chick peas, drained, rinsed

For coconut curry sauce:

- 1 cup coconut milk
- 1 tablespoon tamari
- 2 tablespoons lime juice, divided
- 2-3 teaspoons Thai red curry paste
- 1 teaspoon honey
- Fresh cilantro, to serve, chopped

Method:

1. Add all the ingredients of coconut curry sauce (retain 1 tablespoon lime juice) into a bowl and whisk well.
2. Add carrots, potatoes, chickpeas, stock and half the curry sauce into the slow cooker. Mix until well combined.
3. Close the lid. Select 'Low' option and set the timer for 5-6 hours or 'High' for 2-3 hours or until the potatoes are cooked.
4. Add asparagus and peas and stir. Add remaining lime juice and coconut curry sauce and stir.
5. Heat on 'High' for 5 minutes.
6. Taste and adjust the seasonings if necessary.
7. Garnish with cilantro.
8. Serve over brown rice or cauliflower rice.

Enchilada Orzo

Serves: 3-4

Ingredients:

- 1 small onion, finely chopped
- ½ teaspoon ground cumin
- ½ teaspoon mild chili powder (optional)
- ½ cup canned black beans, drained, rinsed
- 7.5 ounces canned mild or medium red enchilada sauce, divided
- ½ cup frozen corn kernels
- 7.5 ounces canned diced fire roasted tomatoes with green chilies
- 2 ounces cream cheese, cubed
- ½ teaspoon salt
- ½ cup vegetable broth
- 2 tablespoons lemon juice
- 1 cup uncooked whole wheat orzo
- 2 tablespoons fresh cilantro, chopped

Method:

1. Add all the ingredients except cream cheese, orzo and cilantro into the slow cooker. Mix well.
2. Place about ½ teaspoon of cream cheese at different place on the mixture.
3. Close the lid. Select 'Low' option and set the timer for 5-6 hours or 'High' for 2-3 hours.
4. Add orzo and stir. Add more broth if necessary.
5. Cook on 'High' for 15-30 minutes or until orzo is cooked.
6. Sprinkle cilantro on top and serve.

Chinese Barbecued Tofu and Vegetables

Serves: 6 - 8

Ingredients:

- 1 ½ pounds regular, extra firm tofu, press to remove excess moisture, chopped into ½ inch thick pieces

For the vegetables:

- 1 ½ cans (8 ounces each) water chestnuts, sliced
- 3 medium zucchinis, chopped into ½ inch cubes
- 4 stalks broccoli (use only stalks), chop into ¼ inch thick slices
- 1 large green or red bell pepper, chopped into 1 inch squares
- Cooking spray

For sauce:

- 3 teaspoons fresh ginger, minced
- 5 cloves garlic, minced
- 1 large onion, minced
- ½ teaspoon vegan Worcestershire sauce
- 12 ounces tomato sauce, unsalted
- 1 ½ tablespoons low sodium soy sauce
- 3 tablespoons rice wine vinegar
- 1 ½ tablespoons spicy brown mustard
- 1/3 cup hoisin sauce
- 3 teaspoons molasses
- ½ teaspoon crushed red pepper
- ¼ teaspoon black pepper powder
- ½ teaspoon five spice powder
- ½ teaspoon salt or to taste
- 3 tablespoons water

Method:

1. Place tofu on a plate that is lined with sheets of paper towels for a while.
2. Spray the inside of the slow cooker with cooking spray.
3. Place a nonstick skillet over medium heat. Spray with cooking spray. Add tofu and

cook until brown on both the sides. Transfer into the slow cooker.

4. To make sauce: Place the same skillet back on heat. Add onion, ginger and garlic and sauté until onions are translucent. Add remaining ingredients of the sauce to the skillet and heat thoroughly.
5. Pour the sauce into the cooker over the tofu.
6. Close the lid. Select 'High' option and set the timer for 4 hours.
7. During the last 1-hour, add the remaining vegetables and stir.
8. Serve over hot cooked brown rice.

Chapter 12: Slow Cooker Dessert Recipes

Crust less Apple Pie

Serves: 4

Ingredients:

- 5 large apples, cored, peeled, chopped into chunks
- ¼ cup water
- ½ cup raw sugar or to taste
- 1 tablespoon ground cinnamon or to taste

Method:

1. Place apples into the slow cooker.
2. Mix together rest of the ingredients in a bowl and pour over the apples.
3. Close the lid. Select 'Low' option and set the timer for 2-3 hours. Stir a couple of times while it is cooking.
4. Serve warm.

Mexican Chocolate and Zucchini Cake

Serves:

Ingredients:

<u>For dry ingredients:</u>

- 1 cup + 6 tablespoons spelt flour
- 1 teaspoon baking powder
- 1/8 teaspoon cayenne powder
- ¼ cup cocoa powder
- 1 teaspoon ground cinnamon
- Pinch salt

<u>For wet ingredients:</u>

- 3/4 cup + 1 tablespoon rapadura sugar
- 6 tablespoons macadamia oil
- 1 cup zucchini, grated
- 2 eggs
- 1 teaspoon vanilla extract
- ¼ cup walnuts + extra to top, chopped

Method:

1. Grease the liner of the slow cooker with a little butter. Place baking paper at the bottom of the cooker.
2. Mix together all the dry ingredients in a bowl.
3. Add eggs into a bowl and beat. Add sugar and whisk until fluffy. Add rest of the wet ingredients and mix well.
4. Add dry ingredients into the bowl of wet ingredients and fold gently.
5. Transfer the batter into the prepared cooker.
6. Sprinkle extra walnuts on the batter.
7. Cover the top part of the pot with paper towels.
8. Close the lid along with the paper towels. Select 'High' option and set the timer for 2-3 hours or a toothpick when inserted in the center comes out clean.

Peach Crisp

Serves: 3-4

Ingredients:

- 1/3 cup dark brown sugar
- 1/3 cup rolled oats
- 1 tablespoon maple syrup
- 1 teaspoon vanilla extract
- 1/3 cup whole wheat flour
- 1 teaspoon ground cinnamon
- ¼ teaspoon freshly ground nutmeg
- A pinch kosher salt
- 4 tablespoons unsalted butter, at room temperature
- 2 heaping cups fresh peach slices
- ½ tablespoon lemon juice

Method:

1. Mix together brown sugar, oats, flour, cinnamon, nutmeg, and kosher salt in a bowl. Add butter and mix into a crumbly mixture.
2. Spray the bottom of the slow cooker with cooking spray. Place peach slices on the bottom of the cooker. Add maple syrup, vanilla and lemon juice and stir.
3. Sprinkle the mixture on the peach slices.
4. Close the lid. Select 'High' option and set the timer for 2 hours.
5. Serve warm.

Blackberry or Apple Crisp

Serves:

Ingredients:

- 4 cups organic oats
- 1 cup cold butter, unsalted, cut into small pieces
- 4 tablespoons ground cinnamon
- 2 cups brown sugar
- 1 cup walnuts, almonds, pecans
- 2 tablespoons chia seeds
- 4-6 cups blackberries or apples

Method:

1. Add all the ingredients except blackberry or apples into a bowl.
2. Grease a loaf pan with a little butter. Place fruit in it. Sprinkle a little brown sugar in it. Mix well.
3. Sprinkle the oat mixture on it.
4. Place the loaf pan inside the slow cooker.
5. Close the lid. Select 'High' option and set the timer and set the timer for 1 ½ - 2 hours.
6. Serve warm.

Candied Nuts

Serves: 8

Ingredients:

- 4 cups walnuts or pecans or any other nuts of your choice
- 1/3 cup brown sugar
- 4 tablespoons butter
- ¼ teaspoon ground cloves
- ½ tablespoon ground cinnamon

Method:

1. Add all the ingredients into the slow cooker and stir.
2. Close the lid. Select 'High' option and set the timer for 1 hour.
3. When done, transfer on to a cookie sheet lined with wax paper.
4. Cool completely.
5. Transfer into an airtight container and store.

Pumpkin Custard

Serves: 4

Ingredients:

- 1 ½ cup cooked pumpkin or butternut squash
- 2 tablespoons full fat coconut milk
- 3 eggs
- 2 tablespoons maple syrup or honey
- ¼ teaspoon ginger
- A pinch salt
- ¼ teaspoon cinnamon

Method:

1. Pour water into the slow cooker to cover at least an inch from the bottom.
2. Close the lid and select 'High' option and set timer for45 minutes to preheat.
3. Blend together all the ingredients in a blender until smooth.
4. Grease ovenproof ramekins and pour the blended mixture into the ramekins. Keep it 2/3 full.
5. Carefully place the ramekins in the slow cooker.
6. Close the lid. Select 'Low' option and set the timer for 4-6 hours or on 'High' for 2-3 hours or until set.
7. Serve warm.

Gluten free, Grain free Brownies

Serves: 12-15

Ingredients:

- 2 cups almond butter
- 1 cup raw honey or maple syrup
- 2 teaspoons vanilla extract
- 1 teaspoon baking soda
- 2 eggs or 2 tablespoons ground flaxseed mixed with 6 tablespoons water
- 2/3 cup cocoa powder
- 1 teaspoon sea salt
- 2 cups dark chocolate chips

Method:

1. Place a sheet of parchment paper at the bottom of the slow cooker.
2. Add all the ingredients into the slow cooker and mix until well combined.
3. Close the lid. Select 'Low' option and set the timer for 4-5 hours or 'High' and set the timer for 2-3 hours or until the edges of the brownies begin to get brown.
4. When the edges begin to brown, switch off the slow cooker. Let it remain covered for 15-20 minutes.
5. When done, carefully remove the parchment paper.
6. Cool for a while.
7. Cut into pieces and serve warm.

Peanut Butter Polka Dot Brownies

Serves: 20-25

Ingredients:

<u>For the brownies:</u>

- 2 cups unsalted butter, melted
- 3-4 cups sucanat or light or dark brown sugar
- 1 cup Dutch process or dark cocoa powder
- 4 eggs
- 4 teaspoons instant espresso powder
- 3 cups whole wheat flour
- 2 teaspoons vanilla extract
- 1 cup peanut butter chips (optional)
- ½ teaspoon salt

<u>For peanut butter topping:</u>

- 1 cup natural or homemade peanut butter
- 4 teaspoons cocoa powder (optional but recommended)
- 4 tablespoons honey (optional)
- ½ teaspoon instant espresso powder (optional but recommended)

Method:

1. Place a sheet of parchment paper at the bottom of the slow cooker. Place another sheet of parchment paper in the opposite direction. Spray the parchment paper with cooking spray.
2. Add butter into a microwave safe bowl and microwave for a few seconds until it is melted.
3. Add cocoa and espresso into the bowl of melted butter and whisk until well combined.
4. Add sucanat and whisk until well combined. Next add eggs and vanilla and whisk again.
5. Add flour and salt, a little at a time and whisk each time. When all the flour is added, add peanut butter chips if using and fold gently.
6. Pour the batter into the prepared slow cooker.

7. Meanwhile, make the peanut butter topping as follows:
8. Add all the ingredients of peanut butter topping into a bowl and mix well. Make small balls and drop at different spots on the batter.
9. Close the lid. Select "High' option and set the timer for 2-3 hours or until the edges of the brownies begin to get brown.
10. When the edges begin to brown, switch off the slow cooker. Let it remain covered for 15-20 minutes.
11. When done, carefully remove the parchment paper.
12. Cool for a while.
13. Cut into pieces and serve.

Brown Rice Pudding

Ingredients:

- 4 cups milk of your choice, dairy or non dairy
- ½ cup maple syrup or raw sugar
- 1 stick cinnamon
- 1 1/3 cups short grain brown rice
- 2 teaspoons vanilla extract

To serve (optional): Use any

- Dried raisins
- Dried cherries
- Dried apricots
- Dark chocolate chips
- Crystallized ginger pieces
- Shaved coconut
- Berry compote
- Apples slices sautéed in butter

Method:

1. Add all the ingredients to the slow cooker. Mix well.
2. Close the lid. Select 'Low' option and set the timer for 7-8 hours or on 'High' for 3-4 hours.
3. Can serve warm or chilled. Serve with toppings of your choice.

Chocolate Fudge

Serves: 10

Ingredients:

- 1 ¼ cups dark chocolate chips
- 2 tablespoons coconut sugar or honey or maple syrup
- ¼ cup canned coconut milk
- A pinch of sea salt
- ½ teaspoon vanilla extract
- 1 tablespoon coconut oil

Method:

1. Add all the ingredients except vanilla extract into the slow cooker. Mix well.
2. Close the lid. Select 'Low' option and set the timer for 2 hours. Do not stir at all.
3. Open the lid and add vanilla. But do not stir at all.
4. Let it cool to room temperature. Now stir constantly for a few minutes until some of the gloss is lost.
5. Transfer the mixture into a greased tin. Cover and refrigerate until the fudge is set.
6. Serve.

Cranberry Bread Pudding

Serves: 12

Ingredients:

- 9 cups old whole wheat bread, chopped
- 8 large eggs
- 3 cups sweetened, dried cranberries
- 8 cups whole milk
- 2 cups raw sugar or sucanat
- ½ teaspoon salt
- 4 teaspoons vanilla extract
- 16 ounces whipping cream
- 4 tablespoons brandy (optional)
- Powdered sugar to taste

Method:

1. Place the bread cubes on a baking sheet and toast in a preheated oven at 375 F for 10 minutes.
2. Transfer into the slow cooker. Add cranberries and stir.
3. Add milk, sugar, salt, eggs and vanilla into a bowl and whisk well. Pour into the slow cooker over the bread. Press lightly with a spatula until all the bread is covered with the mixture.
4. Close the lid. Select 'Low' option and set the timer for 3-4 hours or on 'High' for 1-2 hours or until set.
5. Beat whipping cream until soft peaks are formed. Add powdered sugar and fold gently.
4. Can serve warm or chilled.
5. Scoop bread pudding in dessert bowls. Spoon some of the whipped cream on top and serve.

Honey Bananas

Serves: 4

Ingredients:

- 2 bananas
- 1 ½ tablespoons raw honey
- ¼ teaspoon cardamom seeds, crushed
- 2 teaspoons coconut oil
- 1 tablespoon lemon juice
- Hazelnuts or almonds to serve, chopped (optional)

Method:

1. Add coconut oil into the slow cooker. Switch on the slow cooker and let the oil melt.
2. Cut the banana into ½ inch slices on the diagonal and place in the slow cooker.
3. Sprinkle lemon juice and cardamom on it. Drizzle honey and stir gently until well coated.
4. Close the lid. Select 'Low' option and set the timer for 2 hours or on 'High' for 45-60 minutes.

Apple Crumble Pudding

Serves: 12

Ingredients:

For the pudding:

- 2 cups almond milk or coconut milk
- ¼ cup raw honey or maple syrup
- 4 cups water
- 4 tablespoons arrowroot powder
- 1 cup chia seeds
- 10 large apples, cored, unpeeled, sliced
- 2 teaspoons ground cinnamon
- A large pinch Himalayan pink salt

For cinnamon crunch topping:

- 1 cup blanched almond flour
- ½ cup coconut sugar
- ½ cup unsweetened apple sauce
- ½ cup shredded coconut, unsweetened
- 2 teaspoons cinnamon
- 2 teaspoons vanilla extract

For garnishing:

- 2 tablespoons raisins
- 2 tablespoons walnuts, chopped

Method:

1. Add all the ingredients of the pudding into the slow cooker. Mix well.
2. Lay the slices of apple over this milk mixture. Do not stir.
3. Mix together the ingredients of the topping in a bowl. Sprinkle this mixture over the layer of apples.
4. Close the lid. Select 'Low' option and set the timer for 4 hours or on 'High' for 2 hours.
5. When done, let it remain covered for an hour to set.
6. Sprinkle raisins and walnuts and serve warm or chilled.

Peanut Butter Chocolate Cheesecake

Serves: 12

Ingredients:

- 3 eggs
- 24 ounces cream cheese
- 11 ½ tablespoons cocoa
- 3 tablespoons powdered peanut butter
- ¾ cup raw sugar or coconut sugar
- 1 ½ teaspoons vanilla extract
- Whipped cream and peanut butter to top (optional)

Method:

1. Add all the ingredients into the blender and blend until smooth. Divide and transfer into mason jars. Cover with lid or foil.
2. Place the jars in the slow cooker. Pour warm water all around the jars. The jars should be covered up to ¾ with water.
3. Close the lid. Select 'Low' option and set the timer for 3 - 4 hours or on 'High' for 1 ½ - 2 hours.
4. Chill and serve topped with whipped cream and peanut butter if using.

Cinnamon Poached Pears with Chocolate Sauce

Serves: 4

Ingredients:

<u>For poached pears:</u>

- 4 ripe, firm Bartlett pears, retain stems on it
- ¼ teaspoon ground cinnamon
- 4 sticks cinnamon
- 1 lemon, halved
- ½ pod vanilla bean
- 4 cups cane sugar or raw sugar
- 4 cups white wine
- 3 cups water

<u>For chocolate sauce:</u>

- 8 ounces bittersweet chocolate, chopped
- 3 tablespoons coconut oil
- 1/3 cup coconut milk
- 2 tablespoons honey or maple syrup

Method:

1. Add all the ingredients except pears to the slow cooker. Stir until sugar dissolves.
2. Place the pears in the pot, standing in the pot.
3. Close the lid. Select 'Low' option and set the timer for 3 - 4 hours or on 'High' for 1 ½ - 2 hours or until tender.
4. Meanwhile make the chocolate sauce as follows: Add all the ingredients of the chocolate sauce into a saucepan and heat until well combined. Remove from heat.
5. Remove the pears with a slotted spoon. Place on a serving platter.
6. Transfer the liquid from the cooker into a saucepan and simmer for a while until slightly thick. Cool completely. Pour over the pears
7. Pour chocolate sauce on the pears and serve.
8. Close lid. Set Manual option and timer for 7 minutes.

Chapter 13: 30 Day Meal Plan

We looked at some amazing and delicious recipes in the previous chapter, now, lets chalk out a 30-day meal plan, which will help you get started on your challenge and at the end, give you results that will kick start your weight loss journey.

Day 1

Breakfast - Honey Vanilla Multigrain Hot Cereal

Lunch - Wonder Soup

Snack - Spicy Black-Eyed Peas

Dinner - Easy Cheesy Chicken Rice and Broccoli

Desserts - Mexican Chocolate and Zucchini Cake

Day 2

Breakfast - Coconut Cranberry Quinoa

Lunch - Italian Zucchini Meat loaf

Snack - Loaded Baked Potato with French Dip

Dinner - Refried Bean Tacos

Desserts - Peach Crisp

Day 3

Breakfast - Pumpkin Pie Oatmeal with Chai Tea

Lunch - Cinnamon Pot Roast

Snack - German Potato Salad

Dinner - Fajita Salsa Chicken

Desserts - Candied Nuts

Day 4

Breakfast - Creamy Homemade Yogurt and Pumpkin Bread

Lunch - Gingered Beef

Snack - Refried Beans

Dinner - Ham Sandwiches

Desserts - Blackberry or Apple Crisp

Day 5

Breakfast - Crust less Spinach and Feta Quiche

Lunch - Enchilada Orzo

Snack - BBQ Chicken Drummies

Dinner - Lamb with Olives and Potatoes

Desserts - Pumpkin Custard

Day 6

Breakfast - Oatmeal with Vegetables

Lunch - Salmon Fillets and Asian-Style Vegetables

Snack - Chicken Nachos with Corn and Jalapeno Dip

Dinner - Pureed Broccoli Soup

Desserts - Crust less Apple Pie

Day 7

Breakfast - Apple Granola Crumble

Lunch - Garlicky Chicken

Snack - Texas Style Baked Beans

Dinner - Tomato Beef and Macaroni Soup

Desserts - Gluten free, Grain free Brownies

Day 8

Breakfast - Fruited Irish Oatmeal

Lunch - Baked Chicken with Summer Vegetables

Snack - Mushroom Garlic Crostini

Dinner - Chinese Barbecued Tofu and Vegetables

Desserts - Chocolate Fudge

Day 9

Breakfast - Huevos Rancheros

Lunch - Lentil and Ham Soup

Snack - Crab Spread

Dinner - Creamy Polenta with Chili Lime Shrimp

Desserts - Apple Crumble Pudding

Day 10

Breakfast - Broccoli, Bacon and Bell Pepper Casserole

Lunch - Healthy Enchiladas with Quinoa

Snack - Bavarian Red Cabbage

Dinner - Moroccan Lamb Shank

Desserts - Cranberry Bread Pudding

Day 11

Breakfast - 3 Cheese Shrimp and Grits

Lunch - Simple Hamburger Stew

Snack - Barbecue Chickpeas

Dinner - Shrimp Scampi

Desserts - Brown Rice Pudding

Day 12

Breakfast - Sausage and Apple Bread Pudding

Lunch - White Beans with Aji Verde Sauce

Snack - Chicken Taco Salad

Dinner - Sour Cream Pork Chops

Desserts - Peanut Butter Chocolate Cheesecake

Day 13

Breakfast - Chili Verde Breakfast Lasagna

Lunch - Buffalo Chicken Lettuce Wraps

Snack - Party Potatoes with Creamy Aioli

Dinner - Farmer's Mexican Chicken Soup

Desserts - Honey Bananas

Day 14

Breakfast - Spinach and Mushroom Casserole

Lunch - Shrimp N Spaghetti

Snack - Baked Potatoes with Pepperoni Dip

Dinner - Asian Short Ribs

Desserts - Chocolate Fudge

Day 15

Breakfast - Quinoa Breakfast Casserole

Lunch - Spicy Black Bean Soup

Snack - Vegetarian Chili

Dinner - Turkey Shepherd's Pie

Desserts - Cinnamon Poached Pears with Chocolate Sauce

Day 16

Breakfast - Pumpkin Spice White Hot Chocolate

Lunch - Black Bean Stuffed Sweet Potatoes

Snack - Spicy Black-Eyed Peas

Dinner - Beef Shawarma

Desserts - Apple Crumble Pudding

Day 17

Breakfast - Veggie Juice

Lunch - Garlic Tilapia

Snack - Loaded Baked Potato with French Dip

Dinner - Carnitas Tacos

Desserts - Crust less Apple Pie

Day 18

Breakfast - Mexican Fiesta Breakfast Frittata with Apple Honey Tea

Lunch - Sesame Ginger Turkey Wraps

Snack - German Potato Salad

Dinner - The Ultimate Chili

Desserts - Peanut Butter Polka Dot Brownies

Day 19

Breakfast - Broccoli, Bacon and Bell Pepper Casserole

Lunch - Chicken N Beans

Snack - Mushroom Garlic Crostini

Dinner - Creamy Potato and Corn Chowder

Desserts - Peanut Butter Chocolate Cheesecake

Day 20

Breakfast - Maple Pumpkin Spice Latte

Lunch - Autumn Vegetable Beef Stew

Snack - BBQ Chicken Drummies with Buffalo Chicken Dip

Dinner - Lemon Pepper Tilapia with Asparagus

Desserts - Gluten free, Grain free Brownies

Day 21

Breakfast - Huevos Rancheros

Lunch - Healthy Shrimp Risotto

Snack - Refried Beans

Dinner - Mushroom Stroganoff

Desserts - Peach Crisp

Day 22

Breakfast - Sausage and Apple Bread Pudding

Lunch - Zesty Chicken with Couscous

Snack - Easy Chili

Dinner - Corned Beef Brisket

Desserts - Cranberry Bread Pudding

Day 23

Breakfast - Oatmeal with Vegetables

Lunch - Chicken, Black Bean and Quinoa Stew

Snack - Party Potatoes with Creamy Aioli

Dinner - Mexican Style Shredded Pork

Desserts - Peanut Butter Polka Dot Brownies

Day 24

Breakfast - Breakfast - Creamy Homemade Yogurt and Pumpkin Bread

Lunch - African Pulled Beef Sandwiches with Yogurt Mint Sauce

Snack - Chicken Taco Salad

Dinner - Spring Veggie Coconut Curry

Desserts - Blackberry or Apple Crisp

Day 25

Breakfast - Apple Granola Crumble

Lunch - Cauliflower Rice Greek Chicken Bowl

Snack - Chicken Nachos with Corn and Jalapeno Dip

Dinner - Smoky Spicy Lamb Roast

Desserts - Peanut Butter Chocolate Cheesecake

Day 26

Breakfast - Honey Vanilla Multigrain Hot Cereal

Lunch - Italian Braised Pork

Snack - Bavarian Red Cabbage

Dinner - Irish Lamb Stew

Desserts - Chocolate Fudge

Day 27

Breakfast - Pumpkin Pie Oatmeal

Lunch - Farmer's Mexican Chicken Soup

Snack - Texas Style Baked Beans with Reuben Dip

Dinner - Asian Short Rib

Desserts - Cinnamon Poached Pears with Chocolate Sauce

Day 28

Breakfast - Crust less Spinach and Feta Quiche

Lunch - Citrus Chicken

Snack - Crab Spread

Dinner - Pad Thai

Desserts - Brown Rice Pudding

Day 29

Breakfast - Oatmeal with Vegetables

Lunch - Sweet Potato, Apple and Turmeric Soup

Snack - Barbecue Chickpeas

Dinner - Creamy Mushroom Chicken

Desserts - Gluten free, Grain free Brownies

Day 30

Breakfast - Coconut Cranberry Quinoa

Lunch - Butternut Squash, Kale and Quinoa Stew

Snack - Mushroom Garlic Crostini

Dinner - Korean Beef

Desserts - Crust less Apple Pie

Chapter 14: Conversion Tables

Reference: http://startcooking.com/measurement-and-conversion-charts

US DRY VOLUME MEASUREMENTS	
MEASURE	**EQUIVALENT**
1/16 teaspoon	Dash
1/8 teaspoon	A pinch
3 teaspoons	1 Tablespoon
1/8 cup	2 tablespoons (= 1 standard coffee scoop)
1/4 cup	4 Tablespoons
1/3 cup	5 Tablespoons plus 1 teaspoon
1/2 cup	8 Tablespoons
3/4 cup	12 Tablespoons
1 cup	16 Tablespoons
1 Pound	16 ounces

US LIQUID VOLUME MEASUREMENTS

8 Fluid ounces	1 Cup
1 Pint	2 Cups (= 16 fluid ounces)
1 Quart	2 Pints (= 4 cups)
1 Gallon	4 Quarts (= 16 cups)

US to Metric Conversions

1/5 teaspoon	1 ml (ml stands for milliliter, one thousandth of a liter)
1 teaspoon	5 ml
1 tablespoon	15 ml
1 fluid oz.	30 ml
1/5 cup	50 ml
1 cup	240 ml
2 cups (1 pint)	470 ml
4 cups (1 quart)	0.95 liter
4 quarts (1 gal.)	3.8 liters
1 oz.	28 grams
1 pound	454 grams

Conclusion

I thank you once again for choosing this book and hope you had a good time reading it.

The main aim of this book was to educate you on the basics of the whole foods 30 days challenge and how it can help you develop a lean body. The diet can be extremely effective provided you follow it for 30 days and keep going until you attain your dream body.

The recipes provided in this book are easy to put together and take no time at all to prepare.

You can get your entire family involved and turn it into a family food challenge. Do not limit yourself to just these recipes and try to come up with new and interesting ones.

I hope you have a good time taking up the whole foods 30 days challenge and develop the body of your dreams.

Good luck!

Made in the USA
Lexington, KY
30 July 2017